PRAISE FOR *RADICAL INTIMACY*

"*Radical Intimacy* is the conversation and guidance that not only helps you, it can heal you. Zoë Kors's innate and delicate ability to navigate the complexity and necessity of sexual intimacy continues to leave me awe-struck—she is a living oracle."

—Azure Antionette, critically acclaimed poet, Founder of Tell(h)er

"*Radical Intimacy* is the book we've all been waiting for to serve as a guide for our most important relationships—the raw and real relationship we have with ourselves as well as with those we love most."

—Felicia Tomasko, Editor-in-Chief, *LA YOGA Magazine*

"Radical Intimacy is a roadmap through the jungle of our fear and long-ing for love . . . into the warm heart of our true being."

—Krishna Das, Grammy-nominated recording artist and kirtan wallah

"Zoë Kors is a profound listener . . . and what is intimacy other than the ability to truly listen without bias and without judgement? This listening comes through in her writing and in her work. I am grateful to have en-countered, grown, and learned from both."

—Christopher Rivas, actor and storyteller

RADICAL INTIMACY

RADICAL INTIMACY

CULTIVATE THE DEEPLY CONNECTED RELATIONSHIPS YOU DESIRE AND DESERVE

ZOË KORS

hachette
BOOKS

New York

Hachette Go, an imprint of Hachette Books
Hachette Book Group
1290 Avenue of the Americas
New York, NY 10104
HachetteGo.com
Facebook.com/HachetteGo
Instagram.com/HachetteGo

First Edition: April 2022

Hachette Books is a division of Hachette Book Group, Inc.

The Hachette Go and Hachette Books name and logos are trademarks of Hachette
Book Group, Inc.

The publisher is not responsible for websites (or their content) that are not owned by the
publisher.

Print book interior design by Amy Quinn.

Library of Congress Control Number: 2021952290

ISBNs: 978-0-306-82660-3 (hardcover); 978-0-306-82661-0 (ebook)

Printed in the United States of America

LSC-C

Printing 1, 2022

I dedicate this book to my original love pod—my father, Rolf, my mother, Bobbie, and my sister, Laurie. Thank you for starting me out with such a solid foundation. We've been doing this a long time and the intimacy continues to grow.

CONTENTS

AUTHOR'S NOTE

My family has graciously granted me permission to share their names and stories. All other names and identifying details have been changed to protect privacy. All pronouns used in this book reflect the ones used by the individuals in real life.

In the interest of full transparency, I am a white, cisgender, mostly heterosexual woman of Scandinavian and Eastern European Jewish decent. I am a credentialed coach, certified by the Co-Active Training Institute. I've trained extensively in hatha yoga, bhakti yoga, and meditation in a variety of disciplines. Additionally, I trained and practiced tantra with the late Psalm Isadora and have been initiated in a Sri Vidya lineage. I've dabbled in Zen Buddhism since I was sixteen years old through my own self-directed study. In the past several years, however, I have formalized that training at Upaya Zen Center, receiving the precepts from Roshi Joan Halifax in a jukai ceremony. Currently, I participate in an ongoing Socially Engaged Buddhist Training with a focus on alleviating suffering before, during, and after death. To that end, I volunteer regularly at a hospice in Los Angeles called Caring House. In my work, I often draw from the various disciplines I've studied. It is through the lens of my identity, education, and lived experience as a white woman that I write this book. I offer stories, concepts, and perspectives from cultures other than my own ancestry with humility, respect, and the recognition of my filtered perspective.

I SEE YOU. I GOT YOU.
I LOVE YOU.

THERE IS A SPECIFIC MOMENT THAT HAS BECOME INEVITABLE IN THE hundreds of workshops I have facilitated. It happens every time, and it goes like this: Each participant pairs up with someone they don't know. The nervous excitement is palpable. I ask them to take turns sharing something that is hard for them to admit, something they've kept secret from the rest of the world and maybe even themselves. I instruct them how to skillfully listen, support, and witness each other. Apprehension gives way to vulnerability. After their mutual share, they look into each other's eyes for a good ten minutes without looking away, and finally I have them say to each other *I see you. I got you. I love you.* This is the moment I am referring to. It's marked by tears of joy, relief, recognition, and appreciation. Having taken an oath of confidentiality and willingly shed any hint of pretense, it's as if, communally and individually, we step into a space that feels safe enough to be exactly *who* and *where* we are—unapologetically real, raw, and rough. It's just us, it's tender, and it's profound. This is radical intimacy.

Part of what makes these moments so powerful is that they rarely happen in the context of our daily lives. How many times have you brushed off a tense interaction with your partner because you didn't want to incite the same argument you've been having over and over again, maybe even for years? What about when you catch a heart-wrenching glimpse of yourself in the mirror in spite of your efforts to avoid seeing yourself naked? Do you have your own version of escaping into a gallon of ice cream and Netflix instead of experiencing the discomfort of your feelings? Moments like these aren't troublesome as isolated incidents, but the collection of them in repetition, over time, creates a persistent low-key disorientation. We skim the surface of our lives pretending there isn't a swirling bog of unresolved energy growing underneath, the neglect of which leads to anxiety, depression, and loss of purpose.

In my many years of supporting individuals and couples as a sex and intimacy coach, I have come to know, firsthand, the ravaging effects of this kind of distraction, deflection, and denial. Maybe you know it too. Has your spouse suddenly announced they are leaving you for someone else after a lifetime together of raising kids and creating a family enterprise? Or maybe you are knee-deep in the aftermath of a divorce wondering how you once loved the person you now despise with every cell of your body. Perhaps you finally settled down with a "good guy," only to end up in a sexless marriage still fantasizing about sex with the narcissistic hot guy. Maybe after years of being with your partner, you feel more like roommates or siblings than lovers. Or have you always thought you would get married one day but just never found "the one"? If any of this sounds familiar . . . Welcome. You've arrived in the right place.

The long-term consequences of distracting ourselves from the practice of sustained intimacy on many levels aren't specific to gender, sex, orientation, or relationship status. Everyone at one time or another has asked themselves if this is all there is. Everyone has wondered how to sustain desire, enthusiasm, affection, and respect for our intimate partners over time. And everyone has, at one point in their lives, looked in the mirror and wondered where the person they used to know has gone. Our thunderbolt, 140-character, hyperstimulating, same-day-delivery, mobile-order-half-caff-venti-one-pump-sugar-free-vanilla-coconut-milk-latte kind of world provides an environment inhospitable to intimacy, with others, with ourselves.

We can talk about truth telling, authenticity, badassery, self-love, self-care, and slaying the day. We can apply the law of attraction, love languages, and every hack in the world. We can do all the yoga, workshops, and retreats we can make time for. But without an underpinning of intimacy, our experience lacks the kind of specificity necessary to truly know ourselves through and through. With intimacy as the foundational principle of our existence, we can build a life based on what we truly need, not what we have been *told* we need, *think* we need, or *think we should* need. No matter who you are and who you like to have sex with, my intention is to arm you with a new tool kit and consciousness for cultivating the deeply connected relationships you desire and the life you deserve.

ON NAVIGATING THIS BOOK

The concepts presented in this book build on themselves chapter by chapter. For this reason alone, it is advantageous to work through the material sequentially. If you are like me, you will pick up the book and blade through it, all willy-nilly, looking for snippets of words and pictures that grab your attention. That's okay! I honor your curiosity. If you are particularly drawn to a certain chapter or section of the book, I offer the following guidance: familiarize yourself with the Radical Intimacy Matrix presented in Chapter 3 as a foundation for navigating the book either in the order it's presented or randomly. This will give you context as you light a match, illuminating various areas of opportunity for greater intimacy and self-knowledge.

ON SAFETY, SUPPORT, AND SELF-RELIANCE

In reading and embracing the practices in this book, I am inviting you into tender territory, much of which you have successfully resisted for some time. Thoughts, feelings, and even somatic (physical) experiences are likely to arise in which you feel vulnerable. Like the safe space in my workshops, you will want to feel protected in your experience. Any transformational journey is deeply personal. Not everyone in your life will understand and be able to support you. In fact, some are undoubtedly invested in the status quo and will be threatened by your desire to evolve and grow. It might feel lonely at times, but the gift is the relationship you are building with yourself and a new kind of self-reliance. Alternately, you might read this book with a bestie or a circle of friends with whom you journey into the world of *Radical Intimacy* together in a supportive community.

ON GENDER

When a baby is born, the first question many of us ask is, "Is it a girl or a boy?" From the moment a child enters the world, we are expected to relate to them as a gender, rather than as a person. Everything we perceive about them is through the filter of our ideas about gender. The binary model of gender expression is a key underpinning of our patriarchal social structure. Sexism is the prejudice, stereotyping, or discrimination on the basis of sex. In order for sexism to thrive, it's required that there be a clearly defined difference between the sexes. As you move through the exploration of the many influences on your sexuality, much of what you are going to be dealing with has to do with gender conformity—how you are supposed to feel and behave as a woman or a man. This is challenging enough for a cisgender person—someone who identifies as a man or woman and was born with genitals that align with that identification. It's exponentially more confronting for people whose gender identification falls somewhere other than solidly in one or the other of the two binary extremes.

In Western culture, we have long operated under the assumption that if you are born with a vulva, you are a girl and will grow to become a woman. And if you are born with a penis, you are a boy who will become a man. Conventional Western culture's historical intolerance for nuance and subtlety has never allowed for the possibility that there might be a gray area here. Reorganizing our understanding of gender to allow for more nuance might not obliterate gender tropes and the way we stack our expectations against what we misunderstand to be innate identities, but it would present an array of options for how we inhabit our bodies. Think about it for a moment. Given the opportunity to explore your own gender identity, would you describe yourself as 100 percent feminine or 100 percent masculine? Would letting go of rigid gender roles shift the way you dress, speak, behave? Societal gender chaos is perhaps a risk worth taking for the benefit of a more diverse set of criteria by which we discern and understand who we are and how we relate to each other.

ON THE COMPONENTS OF CONSENT

No one is entitled access to your body without your permission. Full stop. Consent should be a no-brainer, but somehow it persists as a very murky subject. I am including some basics about consent to support you in the physical intimacy exercises in this book, as well as in your life beyond. Borrowing from Planned Parenthood, here are the five components of proper consent—FRIES.

1. **Freely Given:** Consenting is a choice you make without pressure, manipulation, coercion, or the influence of drugs or alcohol.
2. **Reversible:** Even if consent has previously been given, you are entitled to change your mind with no explanation required. Even if it's for something you've done before. Even if you are both naked in bed. Even if you are in the middle of the sexual act itself.
3. **Informed:** You can consent to something only if you have the full story. You have not consented if someone says they will use a condom and they don't or if they neglect to disclose that they have a sexually transmitted disease.
4. **Enthusiastic:** When it comes to sex, you should do only stuff you *want* to do, not things that you feel you're expected to do.
5. **Specific:** Saying yes to one thing doesn't mean you say yes to anything else.

Couples often communicate in a kind of shorthand they develop over time. While understandable and appropriate, if you are embarking on this journey with your long-term partner, I urge you to err on the side of caution when trying the exercises presented in this book and to step up your level of sensitivity to your partner's experience. To be honest, the same applies to physical intimacy with yourself. Check in regularly with yourself and make sure you are comfortable with the pace and intensity of your exploration.

ON TRAUMA AS AN OPPORTUNITY

Trauma comes in many forms. At one end of the spectrum, it can be a single act of violence that is nameable and knowable or many years of sexual abuse or harassment. At the other end, it can be a subtle but persistent manipulation of our inner dialogue and self-esteem. I have treated a client for whom a single comment from a past lover about her body caused such deep trauma that it lived at the root of her compulsive self-harm behavior for decades after. Our suffering is not a competition. One person's trauma does not diminish another's. The last thing you need to feel is that your wounds are not valid or deserving of your attention. Your body holds valuable information about opportunities for healing. Follow its clues.

As you journey into the world of *Radical Intimacy*, you may elicit what looks and feels like a trauma response. Clinically, this is your nervous system reacting as if the threat that caused the original trauma still exists in the present moment. To determine if you are having a trauma response, look for the classic signs of Fight, Flight, Freeze, or Fawn. There are many techniques available through the magic of the Internet that help you to calm your response and regulate your nervous system—breathing techniques, mindfulness exercises, weighted blankets, and more. I've included a small tool kit of basic exercises for self-soothing on pages 215–217 to use in a pinch. If your disregulation persists, put the book down and seek the support of a trauma-informed therapist to help you process what is triggering your response. Please listen when I tell you that this doesn't mean you are broken. Nothing needs to be fixed. You simply need more care and healing before you continue on the *Radical Intimacy* journey.

ON THE TRIP YOU ARE ABOUT TO TAKE

Are you the kind of person who sets your navigation app to your destination and then takes each turn as it comes? Personally, I can relax only if I zoom out and get a snapshot impression of the entire trip before I begin. If this is you too, here is your snapshot of radical intimacy. There are three *kinds* of intimacy: Emotional, Physical, and Energetic. And there are three *levels* of intimacy: Self, Other, World. The intersection of these kinds and levels creates nine areas of opportunity to deepen intimacy. For instance, "emotional intimacy with self" is an opportunity to master your emotional life. "Physical intimacy with the world" is an opportunity to explore how your environment penetrates you through the vehicle of your five senses—stop and smell the roses, yes, but how do we taste the wind? You can refer to the diagram provided on page 23 to see all nine combinations. I'll be guiding you through these areas with information, stories from my practice and personal life, as well as exercises that will help you embody the concepts you've just learned.

I invite you to dive deep and work your way through each of the chapters, focusing on one at a time, with no concern for how to weave it together into a cohesive system until the end. I urge you to simply be in the experience of each chapter and each exercise and adopt an attitude of noticing, allowing, and accepting. In this way, reading the book and then interacting with the information contained within it becomes your first experience of radical intimacy.

Bon voyage, happy trails, vaya con Dios, dear reader. May you enjoy a richly rewarding, deeply moving, life-changing journey home to yourself.

PART ONE

THE CASE FOR INTIMACY

CHAPTER 1

MORE THAN SEX

URELY, YOU'VE READ IT IN A NOVEL OR SEEN IT IN THE MOVIES, OR maybe it lives solely in your fantasy life. Maybe you've actually experienced a moment of mind-blowing, soul-stirring, earth-shattering intimacy. Your partner looks deeply in your eyes, takes your head in their hands, and kisses you like they are caressing your very soul with their mouth. Your whole nervous system unwinds with a felt sense of comfort, like coming home. Your body melts; your insecurities fall away; your inhibitions vanish. As your flesh hungers to blur the lines of separation, a tidal wave of desire crashes through you—desire to consume each other, desire to feel yourself, desire to merge with the universe in an explosion of effervescent stardust and love juice. There's no room for thought in this madness, no need for interpretation or meaning. This communion exists beyond the masks we wear, the personalities we inhabit, the stories we tell. It's pure, it's primal, and it's delicious.

If you ask everyone you know what intimacy means to them, half will describe this scene or something like it. The other half will tell you about a road trip or a spa day with their bestie, rife with deep conversation and confessions of tightly held secrets. They'll describe the experience of being seen for who they really are—warts and all—and being loved and accepted anyway. In mutuality, this honest sharing of selves offers validation and acceptance, while cultivating trust and self-esteem. When we see ourselves in others, it gives context to and normalizes our own experience. In this sense, intimacy is the antidote to shame, the belief that we are so bad or broken that we are unworthy of love and belonging—two things that are essential to our general well-being, if not survival. As nourishing as intimacy is, it remains one of the most confounding of all human experiences. We long for, look for, and even chase it. We also fear, resist, and run from it. Most of us can point to an idea or occurrence of what we would call intimacy in our lives, but few of us truly grasp its full expression. What exactly are we craving, and why does it make us so anxious? Intimacy is risky. It can feel like we are putting ourselves out there to be evaluated and judged, which, depending on your tolerance for vulnerability, can be exciting or excruciating. Here's the thing . . . our limited understanding of intimacy has the achievement of it dependent on someone or something outside of ourselves. In actuality, the nature of intimacy is vast and readily accessible to each and every one of us individually.

How intimate are you with yourself? Ponder that for a moment. When was the last time you sat still for a few minutes, put down all the devices, and just listened to the sound of your own breath? Do you have a working knowledge of your internal organs and where they are located in your body? Do you bring your full awareness to the experience of eating your food and drinking your water, or are you distracted by your busy mind trying to figure out the details of your life? Let's go even deeper. Are you intimate with your emotional landscape and which skills you use to navigate the (sometimes) stormy skies? What feelings arise when you look at the sunset, and where do you feel that in your body? And when was the last time you looked at your own genitals in the mirror with love and appreciation? All these are facets of intimacy. The fact is, we can meet each other only to the extent that we can meet ourselves. The rules of the game remain the same whether there is another person involved or we are flying solo. Some things look really good and some things not so much. We can't be selectively intimate and experience only the pleasant parts; it doesn't work that way. You're either in or you're out. Intimacy takes courage, and, when approached skillfully, the rewards are worth it. And, as my client Sarah will tell you, the alternative can be devastating.

Sarah hardly recognizes herself. Her puffy eyes stare back at her in the bathroom mirror as she processes the inevitability of where she finds herself. After seventeen years of marriage and two kids—now teenagers— her husband has disclosed that he is leaving the marriage to be with the woman he has secretly been having an affair with for three months. Sarah had no idea. She didn't recognize any clues that her husband's time and presence were somehow unaccounted for. She is shocked yet somehow not entirely surprised. In the past ten years, their sex life had become essentially nonexistent, and their relationship began to feel more like that of siblings or roommates. Somewhere in the trenches of living life, she's lost her sense of self. She feels unseen, unappreciated, and misunderstood, not only by her husband but by her own self. Gazing at her reflection, she wonders where her formerly vibrant self has gone when she wasn't paying attention.

Where *was* her focus? On running a household, volunteering at school, being on the board of directors of a nonprofit, supporting her husband's big career, regular workouts to stave off hereditary type 2 diabetes and the ravages of aging, and mothering her children in a way that only she could do. Like with so many couples, there never seemed a good time to have an uncomfortable conversation. Sarah and Jack's responsibilities were stacked so high and their resources stretched so thin, they could hardly afford the disruption of looking at the parts of their life that weren't working. They lacked the structure and energy to excavate all the relational microtraumas of unmet needs, missed opportunities for connection, dashed expectations, and shifting identities. Instead, they held it together the best they could on the surface with a good measure of what I call the trifecta of anti-intimacy: denial, deflection, and distraction. Perhaps intuitively they sensed that once they had all the artifacts unearthed to examine in broad daylight, they would be facing the inevitable and overwhelming work of repair and restoration. Jack was compelled instead to start fresh with someone new, leaving Sarah to do the postmortem on her own.

Culturally, we are masters of distraction. Our ethos of busy-to-the-point-of-depletion is one way we avoid the emotional undercurrent and blunted consciousness of our existence. If we don't have time to look at our inner world or the larger context, it doesn't exist, right? *Wrong.* And then there's technology. So much of our relating is experienced through our electronic devices. The recent pandemic has taken online interaction to an extreme, where it promises to stay for some time, as we establish and learn how to navigate a new normal. Though there are many benefits to a digitally connected life, heavy mobile device use gets in the way of intimacy both directly and indirectly. Several studies show we receive an average of nearly 50 daily push notifications and check our mobile devices more than 250 times a day. A survey conducted by RootMetrics found that 23 percent of us reach for our phones within sixty seconds of waking, with another 34 percent waiting five to ten minutes. Brace yourself: one study by Harris Interactive shows 20 percent of people ages eighteen to thirty-four admit to checking their phones *during sex*. Ironically, in all of this connectivity, a vague sense of isolation and alienation inevitably creeps in. By collectively opting to go down the rabbit hole of technology-to-the-point-of-distraction, we decrease sensitivity to the nuance of gesture and expression. We numb to the subtle communication that happens in the spaces between words. Our attention span shortens with the manifestation of what neuroscience now calls "screen fatigue." We consume headlines rather than books, watch videos rather than read, get our news on TikTok, get same-day delivery of just about anything. We have grown easily impatient, distracted, and bored. You know those filters we apply to our posted photos to make them feel dreamy and flawless? They are a metaphor for the lens through which we see our lives. In short, our sense of the world, the people in it, and ourselves is distorted, which is problematic because by definition, seeing clearly what is in front of us is an essential aspect of intimacy. I've had my own firsthand experience with the triple threat of denial, deflection, and distraction. I survived my own ten-year sexless marriage when I was in my twenties.

I met Vic the year after I graduated from the University of Pennsylvania. I was back home in New York treating my childhood best friend to a beer and live music for her birthday. The minute I saw Vic walk through the door with a guitar slung over his shoulder, I recognized him. I had never seen him before, but I felt like I'd looked in those eyes for a thousand years. I can't say it was love at first sight—I hardly believe in such notions—but I felt instantly connected to this man in some distinct and indescribable way. Unlike anyone I'd ever been involved with, he was a musician living for his art. He had the energy of a rock star and the lifestyle of a starving artist. He was charming, funny, affectionate, and resourceful. Two and a half years later, we were married at a restaurant on the banks of the Hudson River.

By the time the alarm on my biological clock was clanging nearly a decade later, we had been living in Los Angeles for five years. The band we had formed, with me as lead singer, had had considerable local success, but no record contract. We had just bought a house in the Hollywood Hills with the help of my parents for a down payment. I booked a trip to Hawaii for our seventh wedding anniversary. We had never been on a trip of this kind. We had spent the past decade committing every resource to the success of the band—first Vic's band when we lived in New York and then our band when we moved to Los Angeles—the rehearsal space, the equipment, the recordings, the custom-made silver leather outfits . . . the list goes on. There was never anything left for such a vacation.

Within the first few weeks of getting to know Vic, he had said to me, "One day, I am going to have a daughter named Rachel. If that's a deal breaker, you should walk away now." At twenty-two years old, I found it minorly interesting that a twenty-five-year-old man already had a relationship with his future daughter. It was irrelevant to me, but I liked the name, and motherhood was part of my long-range vision. Nearly ten years later, I found myself booking a pilgrimage to Kona to conceive Rachel.

The Big Island was breathtaking. I read voraciously about Hawaiian cultural history and spirituality. We drove around the youngest of the Hawaiian Islands looking to tap into the mana of the land, the lava, the wildlife, and the history. We were on a mission to channel that energy into the creation of our child. We had about eight days to make this happen. After about four days of stalling, Vic turned and said to me, "If you want to get pregnant, you're actually going to have to fuck me," thereby summing up the dirty little secret about our marriage.

For what was essentially the duration of our ten years together, I was completely shut down, sexually. It must have been good at the beginning, or we wouldn't have been drawn to each other, but by the time we were living together and engaged to be married, there was a noticeable issue. On the eve of our wedding, he was deeply conflicted about the state of our sex life and considering his options. I barely remember the conversation we had about it, but we did go ahead with the wedding and I believe I must have agreed to sleep with him more often. It wasn't his fault. He was a good and generous lover. It wasn't that I had never been sexual; I had freely explored my sexuality in high school and college. I had been masturbating since I was three, for crying out loud. I loved sex! Whatever was going on with me was specific to my marriage or my health. I had a beautiful man, whom I genuinely loved, dying to make love to me, and it made my skin crawl to even think about it. I was convinced something was wrong with me.

Soon after our wedding, I urged my gynecologist to run a blood panel to determine my obvious hormonal imbalance. She gently, but pointedly, told me that I was a healthy young woman and it had been her overwhelming experience that when a woman is shut down in her marriage, it is because of a dynamic in the relationship. I was adamantly opposed to this possible scenario and awaited the test results with bated breath. In fact, her suspicion was confirmed. My blood work was perfect. There was no easy cure for my lack of libido, no magic pill that would provide an easy solution. I was racked with guilt. I felt broken, ashamed, and betrayed by my body. Add to that a growing pattern of request, rejection, and resentment with my husband, and I was paralyzed inside the cycle, unable to acknowledge or address the issue or my husband's pain. I pretended it wasn't really happening, that everything was fine: *denial*. When Vic did bring it up, I found a way to make him wrong: *deflection*. And I immersed myself in my work, our dogs, and eventually my obsession with getting pregnant: *distraction*. The fact that I was trying to get pregnant with a man I resisted having sex with for a decade is some sort of triple axel of evasive coping mechanisms. Well, we did actually conceive Rachel on that island during the one time we managed to consummate our intention, and we would never have sex again.

I had an easy pregnancy and enjoyed every minute of it. Rachel was born without incident. She was healthy and adorable. The first several weeks postpartum were a whirlwind. I had a lot of feelings! Highest highs and lowest lows. In many ways I was rocking it, but emotionally I was struggling. The oddest thing in the mix . . . since the moment I gave birth, I was hornier than I'd ever been. I hadn't been turned on like that since before I met Vic. I was sure something had happened physically or hormonally in the laboring process that resulted in my insatiable craving for sex. By the time my six-week checkup came around and the doctor cleared me for takeoff, I was climbing out of my skin with desire. Relieved to feel that way after so many years, I rushed home to satisfy my hunger with my husband, who I imagined would be astonished and thrilled. As I walked through the door, he came to greet me.

"How did it go?" he asked eagerly, knowing where I'd been.

And then in that moment—the moment I imagined I would be tearing my clothes off and throwing my naked body at him—I stood there unable to respond. Not just with words, but with desire. I took one look at him and shut down. It was as if someone pulled the plug and drained every ounce of desire right out of me. I was crushed. Stunned, too, actually. There I was, standing in the undeniable truth. There was nothing wrong with me. My body burned with desire: to feel my lover's skin on my skin as our limbs tangled in the attempt to consume each other, to writhe in the ecstasy of taking him into my body, feeling him inside me, filling me up, drilling me until we both exploded, and then collapsing in the after-glow. Those six weeks had shown me that I could feel that again. Just not for my husband. I was horrified. Reality was hitting me right in the face. There was nowhere to hide. I found myself a wonderful therapist, and af-ter ten years of not being able to love Vic the way he deserved to be loved, I left him. Our daughter was four months old.

A couple of years in therapy helped me understand a great deal about myself, my marriage, my childhood, and the symbiotic nature of all of it—standard therapy stuff. I grew to understand how I was repeating a certain dynamic with my mother in the way I was relating to my hus-band. I now sum it up decades later by saying in choosing Vic, I mar-ried my mother. That's true to some extent for everyone; our childhood informs the ways in which we conduct our romantic partnerships. We are taught early on what it looks like to give and receive love. Without even being aware of it, we show up to adult relationships with a set of perceptions, feelings, and expectations. I was preloaded with an operating system that required a certain set of conditions for me to give and receive love in a way that felt native to me. Vic filled that role. Vic was the polar opposite of my mother in terms of personality, but he gave and received love in a way that felt incredibly familiar. It's part of the reason we re-main close even beyond coparenting our, now adult, daughter. We feel like brother and sister.

What was missing for me, where therapy fell short, was that I gained no understanding of how my emotional relationship with Vic affected my physical relationship with him. I was still left wondering how a healthy, educated, self-aware young woman who loved her husband had inexplica-bly lost her sex drive. That I had no one to turn to, no one who could help me understand what I was experiencing, set me on a lifelong path and purpose of exploring and discovering the true nature of sexuality. It's only now that I am able to look back and see the micro and the macro of Vic's and my relationship, in and out of bed, and recognize the dynamics that I have since become so familiar with. If I knew then what I know now, would we have had a different outcome? Who knows—but one thing is certain: skillful navigation of our sexual relationship would have spared us both a decade of suffering inside what was otherwise a loving and respectful partnership.

With Sarah's situation as well as my own, it's easy to look at sex as the reason for the end of the marriage. Most couples who deal with issues in the bedroom try to fix the sex, not realizing that it's merely a symptom of a more fundamental issue, never really solving the problem and, in the process, compounding the relational rupture. What lies beneath the surface could be a million different things and is specific to the individuals and the relationship they've built. Each couple has a different and unique set of challenges. The thing that's universal is a need for intimate connection with themselves and then with each other.

The importance of intimacy doesn't exist solely in the context of relationship. In fact, the practice of radical intimacy starts with us. We are available to connect with others only to the extent that we can connect to ourselves. This goes for lovers, friends, relatives, colleagues, and even the barista at the local coffeehouse. In order to share the most tender parts of ourselves, we have to know what it is we are sharing. And to fully see someone else, we have to be able to recognize our own experience in theirs. For all the times you ever wondered if this is all there is, if you've longed for something that you can't quite name or grab hold of, it's ultimately intimacy with yourself that you are craving. Most of us have not learned to be with ourselves fully, either by example, by osmosis, or by school of some kind. In fact, we've been conditioned to place authority outside ourselves in the form of the media, the advertising industry, religion, and family culture. It's no wonder we lose our sense of self as we get more and more entrenched in the complexities of life over time. We become increasingly distracted from our own inner knowing. With intimacy as the foundational principle of our existence, we can build a life based on what we truly need—not what we think we need, have been told we need, or think we *should* need. This kind of sovereignty is liberating, and it feels like coming home to yourself.

CHAPTER 2

GETTING TO THE ROOT

BABY STEPS ARE GOOD. THEY ARE A NECESSARY METHOD OF MOV-
ing from one set of conditions to another. For example, if we want to
create wealth from a modest financial portfolio, it's easy to see that we
need to break that giant leap into a series of incremental steps in order
to eventually reach our goal. In the realm of personal growth or transformation, taking baby steps allows the nervous system to regulate itself
as we form new neuropathways and develop new skills. Imagine working toward eliminating your road rage on your commute home. Staging
your transformation into a Zen motorist, you might begin by resisting
the urge to express your anger by yelling and instead simply observe the
nature of your anger. The next step might be articulating your emotions
as they arise by speaking about yourself in the third person (a common
mindfulness technique): "This is Zoë getting angry that the driver in the
blue Tesla didn't use their turn signal. This is Zoë assuming the Tesla
driver is selfish, privileged, and doesn't care about others. This is Zoë
making assumptions about other people she doesn't know." Once you
master that, perhaps you take on the shift of assuming the best of everyone on the road with you, knowing each of them is dealing with their

own struggles and distractions. Eventually, by taking baby steps, you find you are unphased by anything and anyone on the road. Good job, Sensei.

The problem with baby steps is they often become the easy way out of making any kind of significant and sustainable change. How often have you seen someone excuse behavior that is counter to their goal, like eating bacon after a heart attack, and shrugging as they say, "Baby steps, right?" Or what about when you crave more me-time in your overwhelming life, and you manage to convince your partner to watch the kids for a couple of hours one day so you can take a yoga class. Sure, that's a baby step worth taking, but it doesn't create significant and sustainable change. We need adult steps for that, maybe even radical ones.

I use the word *radical* not because I have been living in California so long that I've assumed the local surfer vernacular. Brah, I'm not some benny trinuh shred like Slater when I'm just a hodad. I choose *radical* because it captures the spirit of what the journey of sustained intimacy is all about.

Radical was first an adjective, borrowed in the fourteenth century from the Latin *radicalis*, which is from *radix*, meaning "root." The earliest uses of *radical* are all about literal roots, hinging on the meaning "of, relating to, or proceeding from a root."

In the life of a plant, a radical is the embryonic root inside the seed. It is the very first thing to emerge from the seedpod and into the ground. A seedling sucks up water through the radical and sends it out to the leaves so they can start photosynthesizing—using sunlight to create food from water and soil. The radical is literally *groundbreaking* in creating a system of nourishment for the whole plant, an obvious metaphor for the opportunity for humans to break through the seedpod of intimacy to provide a system that nourishes their whole existence.

Radical also means *fundamental*. The fact that we need oxygen in order to sustain life makes the availability of fresh, clean air a radical human need. It's not optional; it's fundamental to our existence. In architecture, a building is supported by the foundation on which it rests. We make sure to select materials that will perform their job well. When doing this, we pay close attention to the properties and true nature of these materials, so that they won't crumble under the weight of the structure we are building. If we apply this principle to the constructing of ourselves and our lives, we achieve the same level of integrity if we work from an understanding of the essence of things like the work we do, the food we eat, where we live, with whom we surround ourselves, and, yes, intimacy.

Another definition of *radical* is *progressive* or *extreme*, especially when it comes to transformation. Visionaries know well that it's easier to restore pieces of the status quo after stretching too far than it is to expand further after settling for moderate and ultimately inadequate change. A perfect example of this is the French Revolution in the late eighteenth century when the citizens of France razed and redesigned the entire sociopolitical sitch in a protracted struggle of epic proportions. It was radical revolutionaries who can be credited with the success of the endeavor.

Here's a little history lesson; pull up a chair. In the late 1700s, France was struggling economically partly because King Louis XVI and his predecessor had spent extravagantly on the American Revolution, leaving the government nearly bankrupt. The peasants were desperate, having endured decades of drought, meager harvests, and rampant cattle disease. The existing feudal system meant there were three classes, or "estates." The First Estate consisted of the clergy. The Second Estate was the royals, who didn't pay taxes and had other special privileges, like carrying swords and hunting. The Third Estate was everyone else, which in the years leading up to the war meant 98 percent working-class peasantry and 2 percent aristocracy. The people of the Third Estate were the only ones who weren't exempt from paying land tax, and they got little in return for the exorbitant amount they paid, and they were pissed.

In an effort to restore order and morale, the king summoned a General Assembly to include all three estates. The meeting was set in Versailles for the following year, and in the meantime, each of the estates was to compile a list of grievances to present to the king. Since each of the three estates had one singular vote, the Third Estate could be easily outvoted. Thus, the common people had virtually no voice, in spite of their popular majority. In the lead-up to the General Assembly, the Third Estate began to organize a movement to abolish the noble veto and establish a vote by head instead of by status.

It's not hard to imagine that the General Assembly was a shit show. Everyone agreed that the system was failing, but a collaborative solution proved impossible. Taking the bull by the horns, the Third Estate named themselves the National Assembly and met separately at a nearby tennis club. In what is known as the Tennis Court Oath, they vowed not to disperse until they had a new constitution. Within a week, most of the clergy and forty-seven liberal nobles joined the National Assembly, forcing the king to recognize them in the General Assembly, and talks resumed.

Meanwhile, in Paris, the people got reports from the General Assembly and grew increasingly panicked about a rumored military coup. Concerned they would need weapons to defend themselves, a popular insurgency stormed the Bastille. It was July 14, and this date is now celebrated as Bastille Day, a national holiday marking the beginning of the French Revolution.

In the following months, widespread chaos swept through the country. Years of exploitation had left the peasants furious at their oppressors, and they looted and torched the homes of landlords, tax collectors, and other members of the elite. This insurgency led to the formation of the National Constituent Assembly and inspired the abolishment of feudalism and the adoption of the Declaration of the Rights of Man and of the Citizen, which was based on equal opportunity, freedom of speech, popular sovereignty, and a representative government.

Writing a constitution (i.e., figuring out the new way) was a big ordeal. There were big issues at hand, like how the electoral system should be administrated and if the clergy would be accountable to the Vatican or the state. Most important was the issue of what role the increasingly unpopular and disempowered king would play. On September 3, 1791, France's first-ever written constitution was adopted. It established a constitutional monarchy in which the king retained royal veto power and the ability to appoint ministers. Although many of the grievances of the common people were addressed by the new constitution, it was a compromise at best. Many were disappointed, seeing the change as insufficient—a baby step where so much more was needed.

Stay with me. This is where it gets radical.

A young lawyer, Maximilien de Robespierre, and a club of revolutionaries called the Jacobins emerged as strong advocates for marginalized citizens without a political voice. Made up of the less prosperous members of society, the Jacobins were passionately committed to a much more extensive version of political and economic reform. Unwilling to settle for baby steps, they plotted the downfall of King Louis XVI and the rise of the French Republic. They were adamant fighters for a strong central government, separation of church and state, the end of celibacy for clergy, dissolution of the monarchy, universal suffrage, public education, and the abolishment of colonial slavery.

In 1792, the Jacobins attacked the royal residence in Paris and arrested the king. The National Convention took over the government and declared an end to the monarchy and the establishment of the French Republic. The following year, Louis XVI was found guilty of treason and was executed by guillotine, followed nine months later by his queen, Marie Antoinette, of "Let them eat cake" fame, which she actually never said but which summed up her inability to connect with her constituency.

Like all radical transformation, the accomplishment of a new sociopolitical paradigm came at a cost. The ten months following the death of the king and queen were so violent and chaotic the French refer to it as *la Terreur* (the Terror). Suspected enemies of the Revolution were guillotined by the thousands. Eventually, Robespierre was undone by his obsessive vision of a perfect republic. His indifference to human life in his pursuit of his ideal turned the public and members of the convention against him. He and about ninety of his comrades were executed after one particularly aggressive night storming the Paris town hall during a meeting of the convention. The French Revolution finally ended in that aftermath of the Terror with the approval of a new constitution and the rise of Napoléon Bonaparte, which was another pit stop on the way to the indivisible, secular, democratic, and socialist republic it is today.

What Robespierre believed was that in the pursuit of a new way of being, it is necessary to extinguish that which exists in opposition to the goal. In essence, act as if you are already in your new existence and cut loose anything or anyone that can no longer hang with you.

To be crystal clear, I am not advocating for loss of life. No one needs to be guillotined . . . literally, anyway. But in your process of deepening your experience of yourself, and expanding your relationship with your world, there is plenty that you will need to let go of. You could approach the exercises presented in this book as simple tweaks for having a few more moments of connection. There would be nothing wrong with that, if that's the extent you are available to explore. They would be worthy baby steps. However, this book is called *Radical Intimacy*, because, like France facing a constitutional monarchy versus a democratic republic, sometimes it takes a proper revolution to arrive at the life you truly desire . . . and deserve.

There is a saying in the Sri Vidya tantra lineage that goes like this: If you really want to be with the Mother, you can knock on her door as long as you want. Eventually, she will let you in. But she doesn't just open the door like a normal person. She reaches through the keyhole, grabs you, and pulls you through slowly.

The Mother is the embodiment of the divine feminine aspect of the universe and is represented in this tradition as Kali Ma, whose love for her children is deep, unconditional, and expressed fiercely. She is the central deity to which initiates of this tradition are devoted. Being with the Mother is a concept that could fill the pages of its own book, but in essence it means to live in accordance with the principles and practices of an awakened and embodied life. It's not as comfortable as walking through a doorway into a new way of being. The journey to a new existence is much more like being pulled through the impossibly small space of a keyhole—dark, disorienting, and with jagged edges that strip away all that surrounds you. Very little survives the journey to the other side of the portal, and you will have to ruthlessly evaluate what is worth hanging on to. Ultimately, you will need to release most of what you thought was important. If this strikes you as dramatic, remember that not everything you let go of needs to have claw marks.

So, as you take a deep dive into the world of intimacy, keep your mind, heart, and imagination open. Give yourself permission to dream big. What is your vision for yourself? Who do you want to be? How do you want to relate to the people in your life? What do you want your experience of the world to be? Take some time to get clear and specific. Write it down, journal it, make a vision board . . . whatever your thing is, do it. Whether it's baby steps you're taking or radical acts of intimacy, they'll be easier executed when measured against a big, well-defined vision. You might decide to pause along the way, but at least you will know what the whole megillah would look like should you decide to go for it.

CHAPTER 3

THE RADICAL INTIMACY MATRIX

I'LL NEVER FORGET MY FIRST SYMPHONY. IT WAS THE NEW YORK PHIL-harmonic at Lincoln Center. I am not sure what the actual program was, but knowing my parents, it was likely Mozart or Beethoven—something easily understood by six-year-old ears. I had been listening to classical music as long as I could remember, wafting through the house from my father's Bang & Olufsen turntable and his state-of-the-art speakers. It was one of his only indulgences, and it included a mile-long shelf of precious vinyl LPs—an envied collection of any opera enthusiast. To this day, I can picture my father wiping a tear from his eye as he listened to Maria Callas sing from her deathbed as Violetta in Verdi's *La Traviata*. (Talk about intimacy!) I was more than familiar with the sound of operatic and symphonic music, but somehow sitting there watching eighty musicians collaboratively create one big sound blew my young mind. Suddenly, it became evident to me that the seamless blanket of euphonious sound was actually an impeccably woven tapestry of many threads and swatches.

The unimaginable perfection was created not just by the creativity of the composer, but by the skill and cooperation of each individual player and one masterful conductor.

My first experience of the New York Philharmonic was a watershed moment not just in my appreciation of the arts, but also in my perception of the world. I might not have been able to name it as such in that moment, but what those eighty-some people demonstrated that day lives on as a symbol of what is possible when we structure our self-expression in service of the collective. What also stays with me is the notion that each of us is the conductor of our life—cuing the playful frolic of the woodwinds and the curious contemplation of the cellos, summoning the soulful sorrow of the violins, and egging on the escalating conviction of the timpani and the confrontational crash of cymbals. Life composes the context, and we conduct all the parts. The more mastery we bring to the podium, the more gratifying the symphony. But just like those eighty individuals, the whole becomes greater than the sum of its parts and takes on a life of its own.

THE THREE KINDS OF INTIMACY

Emotional: Emotional Intimacy is the experience of recognizing, articulating, expressing, and accepting the feelings, sentiments, and moods of ourselves and others. The achievement of emotional intimacy is predicated on empathy and a cognitive understanding of the nuance of emotions, as well as a willingness to be transparent and vulnerable. Seeing and being seen is the foundation of emotional intimacy.

Physical: Physical Intimacy is the experience of connection and familiarity with our own physicality as well as that of another. When we are physically intimate with ourselves, we know how our body works, which sensations are pleasurable, and which cause discomfort or pain. Sex is one form of physical intimacy, as is a hug, kiss, any type of touch, or corporeal closeness—think of being in an elevator with someone or standing shoulder to shoulder at a concert or sports event. Physical intimacy is achieved

	EMOTIONAL	PHYSICAL	ENERGETIC
WORLD	Emotional Intimacy with World	Physical Intimacy with World	Energetic Intimacy with World
OTHER	Emotional Intimacy with Other	Physical Intimacy with Other	Energetic Intimacy with Other
SELF	Emotional Intimacy with Self	Physical Intimacy with Self	Energetic Intimacy with Self

when we can tolerate proximity and touch while remaining relaxed and regulated.

Energetic: Energetic Intimacy is the experience of feeling deeply connected to someone beyond the utility of speech and touch. Composed of three pillars, *presence*, *humility*, and *curiosity*, energetic intimacy happens when we are completely attentive and aware of ourselves or another person. The achievement of this powerful phenomenon requires the willingness to disengage from all judgment, assessment, and the assignment of meaning, in favor of simple and subtle observation in each moment as it unfolds.

THE THREE LEVELS OF INTIMACY

Self: You, ye, yourself. The Radical Intimacy Matrix in entirety is built on the foundation of our ability to be intimate with ourselves. The extent to which we can truly see another person depends on how well we can see ourselves. We can recognize outside of ourselves only that which we know firsthand. This is the proving ground of our skills and capacity for connection and communion.

Other: Someone other than you. In this methodology, *other* is defined primarily as one single person apart and separate from yourself. The work we do to cultivate intimacy between friends, family members, and lovers falls in this level. However, small groups of people defined by a common association also fit into the category of *other*—like family, a small group of friends, or a team of work colleagues.

World: Large groups of people and the natural world. This level of intimacy includes our connection with the world we live in beyond one-on-one relationships. Our connections to local community, city, country, the global community, and the earth itself—all exist as opportunities for intimacy. The vastness of the world and our relationship with it might seem like the antithesis of intimacy, but taking the practice of intimacy from the individual to the many, from the personal to the public, from the micro to the macro, is an essential part of the methodology. Like a fractal, the patterns of intimacy repeat themselves at any scale.

In looking at the Radical Intimacy Matrix, you'll see the three kinds of intimacy placed across the top of the grid and the three levels of intimacy up the left side, the intersections of which create nine boxes. Each of these boxes represents a specific focus area. The goal is to develop each of these areas by applying the techniques provided in this book and some that you will be prompted to develop on your own. In doing so, you will be able to skillfully "conduct" your life, deepening your experience of yourself, your relationships, and the world at large. Some of these focus areas might immediately resonate with you, and some might as well be written in Greek. You might have an affinity, say, for *emotional* intimacy with yourself, but for one reason or another, you're not so keen on *physical* intimacy with yourself. Or perhaps you are very comfortable being physically intimate with others, but you resist spending time alone, hating the feeling of loneliness. All of us have areas of intimacy that are more challenging than others, and—you know what I am about to say—the things that are the hardest to face hold the most opportunity for growth. There are good reasons we are underdeveloped in some areas of our intimate lives that have to do with our own outdated coping mechanisms to ensure our survival.

In that way, our continued avoidance of these areas is a clue to places we need healing. The more persistently we neglect them, the more they need tending to, and the more they become backseat drivers of our thoughts, feelings, and behaviors. I had a whirlwind eight-month love affair that is a perfect example of what happens when parts of the Radical Intimacy Matrix are significantly more developed than others. In fact, my experience with Owen was integral to my understanding and articulation of the three kinds of intimacy and ultimately the development of my whole model.

We were introduced at a conference by a mutual friend. Owen was a charismatic man in his sixties. He was just my type: artistic, cool, and a capable flirt. From his shaggy hair to his silver jewelry, I was impressed. We connected on social media, and he promptly slid into my DMs. Long story short, we texted for three days straight and made plans to get together the following week on New Year's Eve, which required some degree of courage because Owen lived an hour-and-a-half drive from me and it would likely be unsafe to drive home in the wee hours given that we, along with everyone else in the city, would be drinking. But after the intensity of our texting, we had managed to squeeze a couple of months' worth of courtship into a very short period of time, and I felt an undeniable ease with this fascinating man. "Let's do it," I said. It was fun, exciting, and somewhat bananas. We spent the night telling stories, laughing our asses off, and having some seriously phenomenal sex. Owen was a skilled and generous lover.

The next time I saw Owen, I drove out to his house for the weekend. He was waiting in his driveway for my arrival with a glass of wine and a rose he had picked from his garden. Owen's home was enchanting. It was peaceful and delightful, and it became my retreat for the next many months. Owen was a real bon vivant. A passionate conversationalist, he had the best stories and the delivery to match. Entering his world was like a psychedelic trip to a mashup of 1920s Paris, Woodstock, and Burning Man. He was the most sensual creature I'd ever experienced. He could eat and drink and suck and fuck like nobody's business. Hedonism was alive and well and living at Owen's house.

One day, Owen looked deep in my eyes and said, "I want to be more intimate with you than I've ever been with anyone. I want to be as intimate as two human beings can be."

"What exactly does that mean?" I replied with great curiosity.

"I don't actually know, but will you join me in the endeavor of finding out?"

"Well, that's an invitation I don't think I could refuse."

So, with unparalleled intimacy as our North Star, we set forth on our exploration. Intimate we were. We stretched the limits of anything either of us had ever done before, sexually. We did things I will very likely never do again. I felt sensations that were new to me, experienced my body in new ways. We would spend all weekend in and out of bed, in various states of nakedness. It felt natural, loving, and reverent. We were wholly immersed in each other for hours on end, oblivious to the outside world, undistracted by any preconceived culturally defined ideas of sex. We were astronauts on a mission, flying through the stars, gathering energy, expanding our awareness. We were fully present to each other in every moment, gazing in each other's eyes for hours, breathing each other's breath. It was otherworldly. It was nourishing. It was intimate. But it was only one part of the story.

As time went on, with increasing frequency, Owen would react to something I'd say and get angry. We could be talking and laughing one minute, and the next he'd be in a rage about something I had said. It was instantaneous, intense, and irreversible. Each time it happened, I found myself down a rabbit hole with him before I knew it, employing all my relational skills to no avail. In each instance, I was at a loss for the source of his rage or even what triggered it. It was telling that when I asked him what he was angry about, he was at a loss too. Partly because it often happened when he had been drinking, but more because when he was in a triggered state, he was unable to articulate his emotional response. There were things in Owen's past that pointed to unresolved trauma. He was a veteran with combat stories that would make your hair stand on end. He was also the child of alcoholics. Though he had lived a productive life for decades, it's possible that some unresolved trauma remained beneath the surface, waiting to be expressed in opportune moments. Potential trauma notwithstanding, there was something about Owen's hedonism that smacked of someone trying to escape the discomfort of unpleasant emotions, while they churned beneath the surface. Because he couldn't tolerate the discomfort of looking at himself and his emotions, they came out sideways—randomly and seemingly inappropriate to what was happening in the moment.

In the end, Owen lost interest in me as I challenged his emotional fortress. I became less and less available for escapism, and, while he was masterful at physical and energetic intimacy, he revealed himself to be unavailable to explore intimacy of the emotional sort. We chalked up our completion to logistical incompatibility and said good-bye, standing in the same driveway in which he had welcomed me into his world eight months earlier. There was no rose this time. The very next week, in the tender aftermath, grieving the possibility of what might have been, my phone blew up with texts and voicemails from concerned friends who had been connected with Owen on social media. In an act that exemplified his lack of emotional development, he had posted a long soliloquy declaring his devotion to his new lover, filled, in his way, with hyperbole and superlatives. The body was still warm, so to speak. I hadn't yet let my friends and family know we had split up.

It's interesting to tell the story of Owen all these years later. I was heartbroken at the time. I genuinely loved him and was hurt, and angry, and most of all disappointed. The whole episode was a defining moment in my education in intimacy. It really was the first time I parsed out the different aspects of intimacy, putting my extraordinary relationship with Owen under a microscope, both in real time and in retrospect. I gleaned the distinction of how a relationship can be intensely intimate and simultaneously disconnected. For all his willingness and capacity for vulnerability in the sexual part of our relationship, he was utterly unreachable emotionally. Rooted in his unwillingness to be intimate with himself emotionally, he was unavailable to me in that arena as well. It was a relationship in high contrast, with some areas buzzing at full capacity, while others were operating at a dull hum. It's from this awareness I began to draw out the matrix as a model for achieving true and dimensional intimacy.

Often, when an individual or couple come to me for coaching, they are dealing with the kind of imbalance I experienced in my relationship with Owen. Caden is a good example. He and his partner, Brett, had been together for more than fifteen years. They were best friends, coparents, and partners in a business they ran out of their home. They even meditated and surfed together daily. Emotionally and energetically, they had it going on. Caden came to me in the aftermath of the discovery that Brett had an affair, and he was devastated. The backstory is that Caden hadn't been interested in sex for most of the fifteen years they had been together. After the first year, Caden rarely wanted to have sex, and when he did it was not particularly intimate—no eye contact, no oral sex, no cuddling in the afterglow. Brett was feeling lonely and unable to express themselves sexually inside the relationship. In fact, they left Caden once already years earlier out of frustration and disappointment at not having their needs met. Not wanting to lose Brett, Caden agreed to prioritize this part of their relationship, and they entered into therapy for two years with moderate results. Over time, things reverted back, and once again, Brett was left feeling unnourished and their need for sexual expression deprioritized. Left to his own devices, Caden would be perfectly happy never having sex again. As he put it, it just wasn't important to him. Brett was conflicted. They wanted to grow old with Caden and share all the wonderfulness they had cocreated. And . . . they just couldn't do it at the expense of their own sexual wellness. Caden's unwillingness to deal with his own sexuality insofar as it affected his relationship and the impact it had on his partner is another example of the potential consequences of leaving one or more areas of the matrix unaddressed. Caden and Brett had some sessions with me in which we laid out all the possibilities for restructuring their partnership and what it would take to keep their current agreements intact. Caden decided to spend some time with me exploring the boxes called "Physical Intimacy with Self" and "Physical Intimacy with Other" to see how it might serve Brett and their partnership. Brett felt patient and hopeful.

When Addison came through my door, she was out of balance in a different way. A lifelong women's rights advocate, she had spent decades as a midwife. Addison not only facilitated natural births in underserved communities but also mobilized government agencies and corporate entities to allocate resources toward expanding women's health-care options, particularly when it came to reproductive rights. Addison sat on the board of directors for three nonprofits and was a regular speaker at both medical and leadership conferences. Let's just say the "Intimacy with World" portion of her matrix was highly developed. Less developed was her capacity for intimacy with others on an individual basis. Actually, her birthing clients found her to be warm and accessible, and those relationships came easily for Addison. She struggled in the relationships that required her to be vulnerable. While she had many acquaintances and casual friendships, she had but two close friends whom she considered to be intimate. From the outside looking in, you would never recognize that Addison suffered from crippling insecurity. The negative self-talk in her head didn't match the appearance of a confident, successful, and engaging forty-eight-year-old woman. When she came to me for support, she was embarrassed to report that she had never had what she referred to as a real relationship—mutually loving and committed. She had had sex a handful of times in her twenties, but it had been decades and she couldn't imagine what it would take to find herself with a lover at this point in her life. She was terrified by the thought. She was deeply conflicted. For most of her adult life, Addison felt that relationships just weren't meant for her. She couldn't quite articulate why, just that she was way too insecure to allow the kind of vulnerability it would take to create sustained intimacy with a romantic partner. Now, as her fiftieth birthday approached, she wondered if she was selling herself short. She had met Finn at her friend's daughter's wedding, and he had sparked her interest. Her pattern was to become infatuated with someone she'd meet and carry on a fantasy relationship with them in the privacy of her own imagination, never making herself available to the possibility of playing it out in real life. Her attraction to Finn, and the possibility of yet one more imaginary love affair, inspired her to reach out to me for support.

Addison and I spent several months exploring the specific ways in which she learned to think about intimacy, sex, and love. We traced her thoughts and feelings all the way down to their roots and discovered a persistent message in her childhood and adolescence that left an indelible mark: Success is a hair's breadth away from failure. If you don't succeed, you fail. It's not a matter of interpretation. There's no gray area. What followed was that Addison was controlled by a kind of perfectionism her entire life. It turns out the same fear of failure that fueled both her confidence and her performance professionally also informed her avoidance of intimacy. She was able to pursue professional opportunities in part because there were many ways to approach a particular goal. The singular nature of a potential romantic partnership sent her running every time. We used the opportunity of dating Finn to work out Addison's fear of vulnerability, rejection, abandonment, and ultimately failure. Slowly and steadily, Addison opened up and let Finn move into her heart and her home.

Jeff Bridges is one of my favorite actors. He also happens to be a Zen practitioner. I was delighted to come across something he said in an interview recently that appears in *The Talks*, titled "Life Is My Guru." He says, "Intimacy seems to be one of the highs of life, whether it's getting to know yourself in a deeper way, or your partner, or the world that you live in." In his book with his longtime friend Bernie Glassman, *The Dude and the Zen Master*, he takes it one step further. "I notice that when I'm generous, accepting, and loving toward myself, all that's reflected out into the world. The more I cut myself slack, the more I don't judge myself for not being other than I am, the more I'm aware of who I am, see it, honor it, and respect it, the more I do all those things for others. I push them less and I respect their different rhythms."

Bridges is pointing to the three levels of intimacy and how forming a more intimate and loving relationship with ourselves nourishes our relationships with the people close to us and in the world at large. Hold and trust the wisdom in this perspective as you begin to excavate all that stands between you and yourself.

PART TWO

EMOTIONAL INTIMACY

CHAPTER 4

HOW DO YOU FEEL?

THERE EXISTS A PERSISTENT INQUIRY AMONG PHYSICIANS AND PSY-chologists about the mysterious and symbiotic nature of our minds and bodies, how our brains, thoughts, perceptions, sensations, and para-sympathetic nervous systems cause or affect our emotions (or both). It's a little bit like a chicken-and-egg situation. The science of emotion not-withstanding, no matter where they come from and why they occur, feel-ings are a very real and powerful part of the human experience. If we are going to be intimate with ourselves, others, and the world on an emo-tional level, we need to have a baseline understanding of what it is we are feeling and why. The more sophisticated we become, the more fully we are available to engage with our world and the people in it. So often when I ask a client how they feel about something, they have no idea. Just as often, they answer "good" or "not good" with no ability to elaborate. Even the ones who are able to verbalize their feelings in more detail tend to do so in big, broad strokes, like, "I am over-the-moon happy," or "I'm en-raged," or "I am so devastated I can't even get out of bed." Human beings live, die, and are ruled by our emotions, yet by and large, we know very little about how we feel and why.

The truth is emotions are legitimately mysterious. *Merriam-Webster* defines *emotion* as *a conscious mental reaction (such as anger or fear) subjectively experienced as strong feeling usually directed toward a specific object and typically accompanied by physiological and behavioral changes in the body.* "A conscious mental reaction" is actually a point of debate in the field of psychology. In fact, there is currently no scientific consensus on a definition. Several theories have emerged over the past century or two, with the majority falling into three categories. Evolutionary theory sources emotions as instinctive skills for our own survival. Physiological theory sources emotions as a result or by-product of what's happening in our bodies. Cognitive theory sources emotion in the way we understand and interpret what is happening to us.

Not surprisingly, it was biologist Charles Darwin who introduced the idea that emotions exist to serve an adaptive role. Fear alerts us to danger, while feelings of love and affection lead us to reproduce. Tuning into the emotions of others increases our chances of survival by motivating us to steer clear of behaviors that threaten our safety. Picking up Darwin's ball and running with it, psychologist Dr. Robert Plutchik fleshed out his psychoevolutionary theory of emotions by identifying eight primary emotions in bipolar pairs: joy and sadness, anger and fear, trust and disgust, surprise and anticipation. Rooted in our own survival, these core emotions can be felt in varying degrees of intensity and can mix with one another to form different emotions altogether. Plutchik developed his model as a tool for bringing awareness to the complexity of our emotional landscape, giving context for the range of emotions we may experience in any given moment.

The James-Lange theory, an example of the physiological theory of emotion, proposes that emotion is the result of a physiological reaction to an event. The physiology comes first, and emotion automatically follows. For instance, "I feel frightened because my heart is pounding," as opposed to "My heart is pounding because I feel frightened." Your heart pounding at the presence of a perceived threat is the source of the resulting fear. The Cannon-Bard theory also falls into this category but addresses the fact that you can have a physiological reaction to an event without a resulting emotion. In other words, your heart can pound because you took a spinning class, and it doesn't make you feel afraid—that context is important in the experience of an emotion. The Cannon-Bard theory suggests that a part of the brain called the thalamus sends a signal to the brain that triggers a physiological response (pounding heart), and the brain simultaneously receives a signal that triggers an emotional response appropriate to the stimulus. Physiology and emotion occur simultaneously.

The Schachter-Singer theory, also known as "the two-factor theory," falls under the category of cognitive theory of emotion. According to this theory, we experience physiological arousal (pounding heart) and then cognitively identify the reason for the arousal. Our individual interpretation of the arousal determines a resulting emotion. Another pioneer in the field of emotion was psychologist Richard Lazarus. At the heart of his theory was the concept of what he referred to as "appraisal." He argued that before emotions occur, we have an automatic and often unconscious assessment of an event and how it might affect us. We evaluate it and assign it meaning. In this way, how we cognitively understand a situation determines our emotional experience.

The thing that's become obvious in my years as a coach, and even simply as a human being, is that the number-one cause of self-doubt and suffering is our own bewilderedness in the realm of emotion. Almost every one of us is walking around wondering whether our feelings are valid, warranted, and appropriate. Do we feel too much, too little, too deeply? Does the expression of our emotions make us too big, too small, too scary? Conversations with my friends and sessions with my clients are so often centered around the emotional component of a situation or circumstance. Broadly speaking, there seem to be two kinds of people. If you are a thinker, you move through the world relying on your intellect to make logical decisions that make empirical sense to you. If you are a feeler, you move through your life using feelings as signposts. I regularly assess my clients early on according to these two emotional archetypes for the purpose of speaking in a cognitive language that's native to them, but the way in which any one of us groks our emotions and processes them is complex and obfuscated.

The ability to navigate emotions skillfully not only decreases insecurity and suffering but also increases our availability for intimacy and connection. Here are my seven pillars of emotional skill:

Self-Awareness: The ability to observe one's own general emotional state and recognize how your feelings are driving your thoughts and behavior. If you are self-aware, you will be able to answer the question, "How do you feel?" with relative ease. You are also tuned into the way emotions feel in your body and the ways in which your nervous system affects, or is affected by, your emotional state.

Discernment: The ability to obtain sharp perceptions or to judge accurately the nuances of your feelings. If you are skilled at emotional discernment, you will know the subtle difference between shades of an emotion and be able to drill down to the root of what you're feeling. For instance, you know if you are angry because you feel hurt or resentful (or both).

Self-Regulation: The ability to manage emotions and delay disruptive thoughts and behavior in the interest of a greater goal. If you can self-regulate, you are able to notice your feelings and not let them hijack your attention to the task at hand. You might even have tools like mindfulness techniques to soothe your nervous system and wrangle your thoughts.

Responsibility for Impact: The ability to anticipate and accept the effect your presence and actions have on others. Taking responsibility for impact doesn't necessarily mean you actively try to lower your impact, but it does mean you understand and tolerate others' reaction to your position or behavior.

Empathy: The ability to attune to, understand, and vicariously experience the emotional state of another. If you are empathetic, you can imagine how someone feels from within their frame of reference. Empathy is possible when you have felt similarly at one time or another, but also because you have the capacity to project what it must be like to be that person having that experience.

Reading the Room: The ability to feel the emotional state of a group of people. The capacity to read the room is like dimensional empathy. Using your powers of observation to understand the collective emotional state of a group of people is an emotional skill whether you are the speaker or audience. Understanding whether you are having the desired impact allows you to adjust your expression or reaction effectively for the circumstance.

Boundaries: The ability to distinguish between your own emotional state and that of another. One of the most confusing relational dynamics is the sorting of emotions when boundaries have collapsed and everyone is feeling everything. When you are well boundaried, you know where you end and someone else begins. This means you can properly allocate emotional resources to managing your own experience or supporting someone else in doing so.

These seven pillars of emotional skill, when developed and practiced, form the basis of our ability to navigate our world and our relationships powerfully, intentionally, and with efficacy. To be emotionally unskillful means we let our emotions do the driving, either actively with unchecked spontaneous reactive behavior or passively when our behavior is a reflection of unrecognized suppressed feelings coming out sideways. We are at our best when we make decisions and take action from a perspective that includes both intellectual knowledge and emotional awareness, when we consider both what we think and what we feel. To that end, it's imperative that we come to know our emotional life with a certain degree of sophistication. In doing so, we increase our capacity for deep connection not only with ourselves but also with others. One of my favorite Zen koans illustrates the power of emotional skill perfectly:

A big, tough samurai warrior once went to see a little monk.

"Monk!" he barked, in a voice accustomed to instant obedience. "Teach me about heaven and hell!"

The monk looked up at the mighty warrior and replied with utter disdain, "Teach you about heaven and hell? I couldn't teach you about anything. You're dumb. You're dirty. You're a disgrace, an embarrassment to the samurai class. Get out of my sight. I can't stand you."

The samurai got furious. He shook, red in the face, speechless with rage. He pulled out his sword and prepared to slay the monk.

Looking straight into the samurai's eyes, the monk said softly, "That's hell."

The samurai froze, realizing the compassion of the monk who had risked his life to show him hell! He put down his sword and fell to his knees, filled with gratitude.

The monk said softly, "And that's heaven."

There is plenty of emotional skill on display in this story. The samurai shows up preloaded for conflict, as he is "accustomed to instant obedience." He's assumed an affect that asserts his superiority and reacts accordingly to the monk's disparaging comments, which he takes at face value. His fury results from what he perceives to be a disregard of his power. His impulse to slay the monk manifests from his unchecked emotional response. Looking into the eyes of the monk as he is about to slay him, he awakens to the way in which his anger creates his own internal hell. How quickly that anger dissolves, giving way to "heaven." In this story the monk not only delivers a lesson in emotional skill but models it as well in his ability to remain unaffected by the samurai's rage (self-awareness, self-regulation). Also, he was able to attune to the samurai's emotional makeup in order to deliver the words that would perfectly trigger his reaction (responsibility for impact). When the monk softly says, "That's hell," he shows an understanding of the way in which the samurai's anger torments him and again when he articulates the samurai's shift to gratitude (empathy).

One of my clients had a similar epiphany. Patrick came to me for support in cultivating intimacy with his girlfriend of eight months. He knew he had a history of holding back emotionally and withdrawing physically from his partner when he felt vulnerable. He was crazy about this new woman in his life and saw a great deal of long-term potential. He wanted it to go right. When he recognized his old patterns presenting themselves, he reached out for help in what he called "becoming an evolved man." Patrick had done considerable work with a therapist, so he knew a lot about how his traumatic childhood had affected his agenda inside his relationships with women and how his need for a lot of "space" was directly related to his sense of safety. What he needed from me was a tactical plan for staying engaged with his new partner and to be held accountable to following the plan. Easy-peasy. Running in the background of our work together was the narrative of his ongoing divorce litigation. There were a significant number of assets that reflected their considerable wealth, much to negotiate. The bone of contention was the vacation home they owned in Vancouver. Neither of them wanted to continue to share the home because the end of the marriage, and now the divorce, had been so contentious. The less they had to communicate or negotiate with each other on their own, the better. They had three kids to coparent; property co-ownership was asking for trouble. As things tend to do when lawyered up, the negotiation of the Vancouver house took on epic proportions. Both parties were swept away in a tsunami of financial records and forensic accounting, which gave way to personal accusations and proper character assassinations. The undercurrent of all this drama seeped into my sessions with Patrick; you can imagine the effect it had on their children.

In one session, Patrick and I were talking about how his awareness of his childhood trauma helped him understand his own behavior and how that understanding allowed him to choose to act differently. Rather than letting his (now unnecessary) survival instincts dictate his behavior, he was able to be intentional about how he reacted to a situation.

"Oh my God," he says.

"What is it, Patrick?" I ask.

Silence.

"Patrick?" I wonder if I should be alarmed.

"Oh my God," he repeats.

"What's going on? Is everything okay?"

"Yes, yes," he assures me. "But oh my God, I am going to give her the house."

I am stunned. And apparently, so is he. This has been going on for years. Both parties, not to mention their legal teams, are highly invested at this point.

"What just happened, Patrick? What's going on for you?" I inquire.

"I don't know, Zoë, but it's like a light just went on. She can have the house. I don't think I even want the house. I think all this time I just didn't want her to have it." He is processing in real time. "I've been blaming her this whole time for abandoning me, and the truth is, I abandoned her too, emotionally. That's not new; I know that. But what I was just able to see is that I am still holding onto the way my mother abandoned me and that I've been taking that out on Lisa."

Patrick and I continued to reflect on his realization. He had done a lot of work on his relationship with his addicted mother who neglected him and abandoned him emotionally, ultimately abandoning him physically by dying in an accidental overdose. The kind of trauma Patrick suffered is programmed right into his operating system. It's not something he can ever completely get over. Like a chronic disease such as diabetes or hypertension, the effect of this kind of trauma is something that he manages. Like the samurai in the Zen story, he suddenly recognized that he had a choice, that his actions had been driven by an unrecognized emotional state that was lurking below the surface. Once he became aware of his misplaced motivation, he stopped needing to punish his mother by preventing Lisa from having the house. In that moment I watched Patrick move from "hell" and take up residence in "heaven," just as the samurai had.

What Patrick encountered in his epiphany might be considered part of what Jung defined as "the shadow." Carl Jung was a Swiss psychiatrist and psychoanalyst who founded analytical psychology. Early in his career he collaborated with Sigmund Freud. In fact, he became the heir apparent to the founder of psychoanalysis. But as Jung advanced in his research, he developed his own theories, leading to a vision that diverged from Freud's doctrines and required him to follow his own path. Jung is arguably the most seminal figure in the field of psychology, creating several well-known concepts like synchronicity, individuation, collective unconscious, introvert and extravert, and archetypes. His work has influenced anthropology, art, literature, and religion. According to Jung, the shadow is the hidden or unconscious aspects of oneself that the ego has either repressed or never recognized. The shadow isn't inherently malevolent. Its power lies in our unwillingness to accept and integrate it, when it can lurk undetected in the darkness, secretly insinuating itself into our decisions and behavior.

Composed mostly of desires, motives, and impulses, we judge ourselves as morally inferior or unacceptable—it's the part of us we are least proud of, the very thing we wish not to be. It is for this reason that working with the shadow represents a moral dilemma.

In his book *Aion: Researches into the Phenomenology of the Self*, Jung says, "The shadow is a moral problem that challenges the whole ego-personality, for no one can become conscious of the shadow without considerable moral effort. To become conscious of it involves recognizing the dark aspects of the personality as present and real. This act is the essential condition for any kind of self-knowledge."

In Patrick's case, he didn't like the part of himself that suffered the effects of his miserable childhood. That version of himself was angry and withdrawn. He had many historical examples of his shadow self behaving in a way that he later regretted. He felt shame about some of the vindictive things he had said and done in the past, particularly in his relationships with women. It was painful for him to imagine himself as a person who could have acted in ways he judged as unacceptable. In this way, he was at odds with himself. It presented a moral dilemma for him to explore his shadow, because he didn't like what he found. It's part and parcel of shadow work that it challenges the very notion of who we think we are. If we are going to achieve intimacy with ourselves, we need to be present to what exists, not just in our carefully crafted, outward-facing persona, but in the depths of our inner being.

By the time Patrick came to me, he had already come face-to-face with the part of himself he called "Angry Guy" and worked with a therapist to process and integrate it. His ability to let go of the Vancouver house so quickly was a reflection of his familiarity with what happens when Angry Guy runs the show. The sudden realization that that's exactly who's been calling the shots in the house negotiation made it easy for him to let go. In a world where Patrick and "Angry Guy" want two different things, as long as that conflict is brought into consciousness, Patrick wins. His instantaneous pivot is a testament not only to the value of doing this kind of work, but also to the iterations of evolution that are possible when we adopt self-reflection as a lifestyle.

Emotional intimacy with ourselves enables us to navigate our lives consciously. We are less likely to be operating from our own version of "Angry Guy," slaying innocent monks out of unmanaged impulses that often hold our reasonable selves hostage. Our sense of self is much richer when we are able to articulate how we feel, in all its potency and complexity. Our self-awareness in this way is the foundation of emotional intimacy with others and the world. Recognizing our own experiences in the experiences of others is the basis of empathy. It makes us better partners, parents, daughters and sons, friends, colleagues, and customers. It makes us better humans.

CHAPTER 5

LICKING HONEY FROM THE RAZOR'S EDGE

N 1944, THE GREAT ENGLISH AUTHOR W. SOMERSET MAUGHAM PUB-
lished a novel titled *The Razor's Edge*. Traumatized by his experiences in
World War I, American pilot Larry Darrell suffers an existential crisis
and finds himself on somewhat of a spiritual path to find transcendent
meaning to his life. At the start of his story, Maugham quotes a translation of the ancient Hindu scripture, the *Katha Upanishad*. "The sharp
edge of a razor is difficult to pass over; thus the wise say the path to Salvation is hard." Both Maugham and the original text use the thinness of
a razor blade as a metaphor for the ruthless path to enlightenment. It's
a familiar cultural reference when talking about a pursuit that involves
great risk of going off course, landing in one of two extremes. For example: When I am sleep deprived I am often walking the razor's edge between utter brilliance and ineptitude. (This is true!) Or . . . as the country
becomes increasingly polarized, our future is balanced on a razor's edge
between Right and Left ideology. Whether you have set your sights on

achieving "salvation" or "enlightenment," the pursuit of intimacy as both a practice and a skill involves walking a razor's edge—especially when it comes to getting intimate with emotional suffering. As we travel from one state of consciousness to another—confusion to awareness—the path is razor thin with a high likelihood of falling to one side or the other. One lapse in focus, and you end up either in the quicksand of self-pity or in the fire pit of anger. The razor-thin path between the two is traversed by being with the suffering, simply sitting with curiosity in the discomfort.

"Magic happens outside your comfort zone," says the ubiquitous meme in our newsfeeds that's meant to convince us of the benefits of embracing discomfort. There's nothing wrong with a grilled cheese sandwich or a perfect bowl of mashed potatoes, a cashmere sweater or a big downy pillow under your head. The wisdom in this quote isn't about seeking solace in comfort food or a soothing environment. It's about the price we pay— the magic we sacrifice—for intentionally avoiding emotional discomfort. We skim the surface, never really getting intimate with the truth of what we are feeling. Meeting pain head-on is essential to our overall well-being. Left unaddressed, emotional suffering comes out sideways in the form of addiction, disease, or aggression. Remember Owen, the veteran whose unprocessed trauma erupts in alcohol-fueled rage? He's a textbook case of this sort of sideways release valve.

Generally speaking, most of us are perfectly willing to experience joy, hope, confidence, and other feelings we consider positive. It's "negative" emotions like anger, fear, guilt, despair, jealousy, and humiliation we try erroneously to escape. Pain and sadness exist whether we acknowledge them or not. So do joy and contentment. If we numb the emotions we call negative, the ones we call positive go with them. We cannot pick and choose emotions. We either fully feel them all or dull them all.

For many people, there is plenty of cultural reinforcement of the delusion that things like betrayal, divorce, accidents, illness, and loss shouldn't happen to us. That if they do, it's unfair or something is wrong. That we deserve to feel only ease and comfort. The cultural phenomenon of striving to only feel good is splattered across T-shirts in statements like "No bad days" and "Good vibes only." The idea that a life best lived is one in which each happy moment seamlessly follows the next is not only unrealistic but a symptom of privilege and entitlement. For some of us, the degree of hardship and discomfort we deal with daily is far greater than for others and depends largely on the circumstances we were born into. For a child who struggles with food insecurity, "No bad days" is not an option. For a person who is neurodivergent, "Good vibes only" may not be possible. If we are going to live intimately with ourselves and those around us, it's crucial to recognize that the amount of suffering in the world is not evenly distributed. If you find you are among the ones carrying a lighter load, you might consider making a commitment to relieve the suffering of someone who is carrying more. Make no mistake, though, even the most well resourced among us will inevitably face hardship of some kind and emotional turmoil. To some extent, we are complicit in the cooperative delusion that it's not fair when life throws us curveballs. What if we flipped that narrative on its head and started believing that there's an opportunity inherent in the challenges of disappointment, rejection, and loss? That feelings aren't good or bad, that they just are what they are? That every challenging experience is a potential rite of passage? That we are willing participants in the creation of the kind of magic our newsfeeds advise is possible? Whether we are the victims of illness, discrimination, disaster, circumstance, or the bad behavior of a friend, lover, colleague, or family member, there is a built-in opportunity to seek out and discover our inner resource, to leverage pain in finding strength. There are times when the only agency we have is over how we feel. In these moments, our choice—and ultimately our integrity—depends on the breadth of emotion we allow ourselves to feel.

As Buddhist teacher Pema Chödrön says, "Only to the extent that we are willing to expose ourselves over and over again to annihilation, can that which is indestructible in us be found."

Over the years of observing myself, my loved ones, and my clients, I have come to understand the three core ways in which we avoid feeling the discomfort of our emotions, which I referenced in Chapter 1 as the *trifecta of anti-intimacy:* denial, deflection, and distraction.

DENIAL

Pretending there isn't a problem at all, we convince ourselves (and others) that everything is A-OK. Living in denial of emotional pain causes cognitive dissonance—telling ourselves what we feel doesn't really exist. It's a lot like gaslighting ourselves. *Gaslighting,* taken from the 1944 film of the same name, has been used to describe the manipulative behavior of narcissists who systematically disable the people close to them by invalidating their experience, understanding, and memories of conversations and events. Those being gaslit will often ask themselves, "Am I crazy?" as they try to figure out why their internal navigation system doesn't match their external reality. When we deny our own feelings, we are both the abuser and the abused. We alienate our cognitive selves from our emotional selves. We disconnect from our intuition, losing trust in ourselves and our ability to accurately discern what is real.

Here is one example of what denial can look like:

Bobby's wife never wanted to have sex with him anymore. That's how he put it when he came to me for help.

"Bobby, what do you think is really going on?" I inquire.

"Well, I think my wife has suddenly lost her sex drive," he says.

"Does she self-pleasure?"

"Do you mean masturbate?"

"Uh, yes."

"She has a vibrator, and I know she uses it." He sounds less than happy about this fact.

"So, she hasn't lost her sex drive."

"So then why doesn't she want to have sex with me?" he asks with a distinct lack of defensiveness.

"Have you asked her?"

"I've tried to, but it's a little bit like the elephant in the room," he says.

"You've been together for twelve years. What was it like in the beginning?"

"Well, if I'm honest about it, it's never been great. For the first couple of years, we had sex about once every week or two, and I always had to initiate. She never really seemed to fully get into it. She said she enjoyed having sex, but it never felt like it to me."

"So, when you say your wife suddenly lost her sex drive, it's actually not sudden at all . . ."

"I guess not."

"And we know she is able to connect with *herself* sexually."

"Right, so what you are saying is that I am the problem."

"No, Bobby. I am saying that the elephant in the room didn't suddenly just show up. You've been feeding and watering it for many years."

"God, you're totally right. What do I do now?"

"You have an open and honest conversation about the elephant."

Bobby went on to talk about how during the first year they were dating, it felt important to him that they have a good sex life. They had tons of chemistry outside the bedroom, and he felt like the sex was good enough. He thought it would get better with time. And at the bottom of it all, he feared he wasn't a good-enough lover for his wife. He felt inadequate and embarrassed to hear what he feared was the truth. So, he buried his feelings so deep, he forgot they were there and created a world in which all was fine. He lived in that world until the cognitive dissonance became undeniable. Infrequent sex became no sex, and he was forced to look at where he had been for the past twelve years. Getting to the root of their dynamic was all the more challenging because of the years it went unaddressed. Had Bobby been able to face his discomfort when he initially felt it, he might have saved himself years of loneliness inside his marriage. In sitting with his discomfort, he might have come to understand his fear of not being enough. With compassion for himself, he might have found the courage to confront his wife and share his feelings. He might have been able to get past his own concerns and be curious about what was going on for her and how he could better meet her needs. His (and as it turns out his wife's) denial of what was actually happening robbed them of the possibility of a mutually satisfying sexual connection.

DEFLECTION

Unwilling to take responsibility for our own experience, we direct our pain at someone or something else. In deflecting, our original emotion often gets distorted past recognition, making it hard to track what is actually happening.

Here is one example of what deflection can look like:

Kim's husband, John, left her after revealing he had fallen in love with one of his colleagues. He had known Stacy for several years, and Kim had actually met her several times at company events. John's announcement was shocking. There was nothing that indicated something had shifted in their dynamic or that he might be having an affair. Devastated, Kim asked him to immediately move out of their home. In the months that followed, Stacy became the focus of Kim's emotional energy. She spent hours on social media in an activity I call "pain shopping," scouring everything she could find about the woman she considered the rival to whom she had lost. She called her names, like "the Whore" and "Stanky." She criticized her education, her clothing, her friends. Anything she could find about Stacy became ammunition for decimating her. Kim was livid, and she was obsessed.

"You have sustained a serious trauma, Kim. I want to validate how painful this is for you," I offer during one of our sessions.

"I can't believe this is happening to me," she replies. "I am a living, breathing cliché."

"And yet, here you are."

"I can't believe John chose her over me. I have so much more on the ball than that skank does. What the actual fuck is he thinking?" Kim is angry.

"I am not sure decisions like this are made by thinking as much as feeling."

"John doesn't have feelings. He is all intellect. He's an emotional idiot. Somehow that whore said something that made him think he would be better off with her. She tricked him into choosing her."

"Do you think that's true, Kim?" I ask. "Do you think it's at all possible that John developed genuine feelings for Stacy?"

Silence.

"Kim? What's coming up for you?"

For the first time in the three or four months I have been working with her, Kim begins to sob. She cries so hard she can't talk. She is finally touching the root of her pain.

It was excruciating for Kim to sit with the feeling of abandonment. By leaving Kim so abruptly, John was poking a stick at the wound she had sustained in childhood. It was the very thing she lived in fear of, and here it was. The feeling of abandonment was so difficult for Kim to be with that she deflected her pain into anger at Stacy. She wasn't nearly as angry at John as she was at the new object of his desire. The rejection she felt was assuaged by tearing down her competition, a contest she created in her own mind so that she could win, over and over. When she allowed herself to entertain the possibility that John hadn't been tricked into leaving her, that he had actually fallen in love with someone else, the floodgate opened, and reality poured in. Kim was able to look at her own pain—abandonment, rejection, betrayal, grief, fear. What came next was her exploration of things she had contributed to their dynamic that led John to craving the kind of connection he ended up finding outside the marriage. Don't get me wrong here. I am not saying it was actually Kim's fault that John left her, but she herself needed to work through that piece too and take responsibility for the person she had become inside her marriage. There was a lot for Kim to unpack and explore—and it was not easy or comfortable. You could try to make an argument that it would have been easier for Kim to stay absorbed in her anger at Stacy. But she would have missed the opportunity to meet herself in her most tender, vulnerable place and truly heal ancient wounds along with the fresh ones. Besides, how comfortable do you think it is to carry such anger and vitriol?

DISTRACTION

In order not to feel pain, we often distract ourselves with things that are inherently unhealthy, like eating, drinking, sex, shopping, or other compulsive behaviors. However, this isn't always the case. Sometimes we allocate an abundance of resources like time and energy toward the wonderful and nourishing areas of our lives, to an extent that prevents deep healing work and the disruption and discomfort it brings. You'll see this kind of distraction take the form of a workaholic, an exercise fanatic, or a mother who is so obsessed with her child that she sacrifices all of her needs and forfeits a life of her own. Distractions can appear destructive or be disguised as benevolent attributes. The distinction is often in the subtleties.

Here is one example of what distraction can look like: You have likely heard some version of Nia's story. Nia, a dear friend of mine, owns and runs a thriving business in Los Angeles. She is at the top of her game and successful by any criteria you might measure such things. Not only that, but she is gorgeous inside and out. She is the kind of person who lights up a room, whether it's a boardroom or a bar. In addition to her professional accomplishments, when Nia was nearing her forties with no relationship in sight, she decided to have a baby on her own. With the help of a sperm donor, she now has an adorable little son who lights up a room the same way his mommy does.

Much to her own disappointment, the one thing Nia hasn't created in her life is a romantic partnership. As confident and secure as she is in all areas of her life, she is equally insecure when it comes to the men she dates. In the past few years, she has given up her pursuit of a relationship entirely. Nia knows that the kind of relationship she would want to have would require her to address some of the deep-seated trauma she suffered earlier in her life that has thus far gone untouched. Meeting a partner fully would require her to meet herself. She would also need to make room for a partner in her busy life. Nia runs on perpetual overwhelm. She is in constant motion from the moment she wakes until her head hits the pillow. She never drops a ball in her professional life, nor with her son, and she is one of the most devoted friends I've ever had. A romantic partnership might be the thing that tips the apple cart, requiring an overhaul of Nia's skillfully stacked priorities. I've often wondered whether Nia doesn't have a partner because she is so busy or if she is so busy so she doesn't have to deal with the emotional discomfort of a relationship.

If embracing the experience of our own pain is challenging, inflicting pain on others is exponentially hard. Taylor and Sam had been together since they were teenagers. They were drawn to each other in their shared childhood trauma. Now in their thirties after eighteen years together, their personal and professional lives were enmeshed. Together, they had built a thriving business and a home. From the outside looking in, it was a pretty picture, one that didn't show the way Taylor had stopped sleeping with her wife and was shut down sexually in her marriage. When she heard me tell the story of my own sexless marriage on a podcast, describing how Vic felt more like my brother than my husband, it resonated with her. She reached out to book a discovery session. In our first conversation, Taylor revealed that she had been sober for nearly the entire marriage. Sam had just quit drinking earlier that year and had done a thirty-day program in a residential rehab facility. After more than a decade numbing the effects of her childhood trauma, Sam now felt everything. She was short-tempered and angry, then sad and withdrawn, then remorseful and affectionate. Sam alternately projected her anger onto Taylor, erroneously pointing to her as the cause of her misery, and then putting her on a pedestal, apologizing for her bad behavior. Additionally, Sam's mood swings were affecting their business, and Taylor was taking up the slack for her emotionally debilitated partner. Taylor was a superstar. She was one of those people you would call in when you wanted to get something done well. She could keep all the plates spinning while cooking you a grilled cheese sandwich and making you laugh. It wasn't a surprise that she held their life together while Sam fell apart. Taylor was filled with understanding and compassion for her wife, but it was a lot to hold.

Taylor came to our first conversation hungry for validation. "I thought I was completely shut down sexually, that there was something wrong with me. I travel frequently for work, and in the last year, I've met several people that I have an instant chemistry with. I feel like everywhere I go, there is someone I wish I could have sex with."

"Have you acted on that urge?" I ask gently.

"No, I haven't. But I am afraid that unless something changes, I will. I feel like such a bad person," she replies.

"First of all, this is our private space. I give you permission to be exactly who you are and feel exactly as you do. There is no judgment here, and these sessions are completely confidential. You are not a bad person; you are just a person living a life and trying to do the best you can. I invite you to speak freely in this 'laboratory of Taylor.' We can always take something back if after we look at it, it no longer feels true."

"Thank you, thank you. That's good to hear."

"Tell me about the beginning of your relationship. How was the sex?"

"It was good for the first few years. I mean, it was good for who I was at that time, if that makes sense. I am not sure I would be with Sam if we met today. I have grown so much since then. We were kids!" she says.

"It does make sense, and you're not alone in feeling this way. This is true for many couples," I offer. "Was there a point at which the sex was no longer satisfying?"

"As Sam started drinking more, she was often preoccupied, or just plain drunk. Sex became less frequent and less intimate. I often went to bed before her, and by the time she came in I was asleep. Sometimes I just pretended to be asleep," she confesses.

Taylor went on to tell me that Sam made the decision to get sober when she started adding vodka to her orange juice in the morning. It was a wake-up call that she was out of control. She decided to go to an inpatient program because she felt she needed to remove herself from her environment while she stabilized. Because of their family histories, both women were familiar with the available options for treating addiction, and they made that decision together. Taylor had grown up in Al-Anon, then later worked her own steps, attending AA meetings in support of her own sobriety. She had a high level of self-awareness in this arena. As she said to me, "I am the poster child for codependency." She spoke about Sam's history and resistance to dealing with her issues, how that affected their relationship, and how ultimately she felt like she was Sam's mother. She felt like the only adult in the relationship. She had hoped that it would get better after rehab, but those hopes were dashed when Sam came home riding an emotional roller coaster. Taylor felt like Mommy now more than ever. She was exasperated, angry, hurt by the way Sam's neediness had stifled her life. She was tired of taking care of her, and she rarely felt taken care of in return. She longed for a solid, steady partner she could lean into.

After listening to her intently for almost an hour, I say, "Taylor, let me go out on a limb here."

"Oh my God, okay, what?" It's almost as if she is anticipating what I am about to say and isn't sure if she is ready to hear it.

"In your heart of hearts, I think you know that you want to leave your marriage."

Taylor sighs deeply. "I do. I don't want to be here anymore. I fantasize all the time about leaving. I am done. I am really done."

"Why do you stay?"

"Because I don't want to hurt Sam. It would destroy her if I left, and I can't bear to do that to her." Said like a true codependent.

"I know what that feels like. It really sucks to hurt someone. What if I told you, you were hurting Sam by staying?"

"What do you mean?" Curiosity peeks through her deflation.

"You are not happy and fulfilled in this marriage, and you haven't been for many years. You've stayed way past its expiration date trying to make it work and encouraging Sam to do her work to deal with her trauma and heal her wounds. She has just now, after eighteen years, started her process of doing so."

"You're right. All that time she was drinking, she wasn't doing her work," Taylor says.

"Right. And when you are in the disease, you cannot be relational. Sam's drinking wasn't a problem for the first several years, but I can see that you have been doing all of the emotional heavy lifting from the start."

"Yes, totally." She is realizing why she feels so exhausted and turned off.

"So why do you stay?"

"Because I can't bear to hurt her."

"What if I told you your need to be the good guy is selfish?"

"You're blowing my mind."

"And what if I told you that it's not the worst thing in the world to hurt Sam?"

"It feels like the worst thing," she moans.

"I know. It sucks to cause someone pain. Listen, Sam is hurting all on her own. By leaving her, you give her an opportunity to meet herself. You also give her the opportunity to meet a partner who can love her in the way that she deserves."

"My dream is that she would finally do her work and heal if I wasn't around. Our relationship is so entangled, I don't even understand it completely, but somehow my presence enables her to be half alive."

"That's a good description of what can happen with codependency. Neither partner is emotionally independent (hence the name), the boundaries collapse, and they take on the responsibility of each other's emotional life," I explain.

"Zoë, I can't do this anymore. I need to individuate." Clarity is arriving.

"I hear that," I say. "I know it sounds like a Hallmark card, but it is often in the loss of a lover that we find ourselves."

"Ahhh, I love that."

Taylor and I spent the next three months exploring what it would mean to dissolve her partnership with Sam on all levels. There was a business to manage, a house to sell, dogs to care for, and belongings to divide. We spent a good deal of time unraveling Taylor's guilt about hurting Sam and finding her own grief at the loss of so much she had invested in. She had created her whole adult life with Sam. Letting it go was a process that deserved care and attention. When the time came, it was gut wrenching for Taylor to tell Sam she was leaving, for both of them. Sam was devastated and fought it at first, cycling through the five stages of grief, acting them out demonstratively. But she had a strong support system in her sober community, and, eventually, she was able to accept what was happening. She had her own revolution of self. In the end, Taylor learned that it wasn't that she handed Sam her life back *even though* she hurt her, but *because* she hurt her.

In tantra, a spiritual philosophy known for its sensuality, there is a saying: "Life is licking honey from the razor's edge and tasting the sweetness as it cuts you." In other words, when we do life right, we are so intimate with the path itself that instead of walking it, we lick it. The simultaneity of pain and pleasure is part of the experience. Both are inevitable and inextricably linked. Emotional pain can be a treasured friend and teacher, if met with curiosity and a willingness to engage with it.

I could tell you that every cloud has a silver lining and that what doesn't kill you makes you stronger. But this isn't about finding silver linings or assigning some kind of meaning to your hardships. This is about choosing not to delude yourself into thinking pain is optional. This is about having the courage to be honest with yourself about what you are experiencing. It's not about always staying positive by denying what doesn't feel good. It's about walking straight into the center of discomfort and staying there, peeling back one layer of awareness at a time until you get to the very marrow of your own existence. Because you know what? That is what it means to be truly alive, to be intimate with ourselves no matter what, to love ourselves unconditionally, through thick and thin, in sickness and in health, till death do us part.

CHAPTER 6

EMOTIONAL INDEPENDENCE

IMAGINE THAT YOU FIND A SENSE OF WHOLENESS IN YOURSELF. You've got your feet on the ground and your face turned toward the sun. You feel confident and at ease in your own being and in the way you relate to others. At any given moment you know how you feel, or you know how to figure out how you feel. You have clear boundaries, which means you're not taking on other people's emotional labor and you are not blaming others for the way you feel. You are aware of the way your words and behavior affect those around you. You anticipate and adjust your expression so that you are not creating unnecessary misunderstandings and messes that you will need to clean up later. This is *emotional independence*, which I define as the state of dominion over one's emotional life, without conscious or unconscious reliance on the input of others to regulate one's mood, the ability to self-reflect, self-soothe, and self-regulate. There are three key aspects of emotional independence: cultivating witness consciousness, owning your shit, and taking responsibility for impact.

I remember one of my earliest experiences that laid the groundwork for what I now recognize as emotional independence. I spent the entirety of my childhood with birds inside our home. At any given time, we had either a pet parrot, parakeet, finches, or a cockatiel. At one point, when I was in college, my parents even built an aviary and bred canaries. I have a special fondness for birds as a result. When I was six years old, my family had a green and yellow parakeet. Barney liked to walk around on the kitchen floor like a dog, catching crumbs and hitching an occasional ride on a passing foot. One day after school, my father, Rolf, and I were rushing around making a snack on the way out to my ballet class. I was in my black leotard and brown leather sandals—the ones we got on vacation in Cape Cod from a real leathersmith, with big flat waffle-patterned rubber soles. I cannot report the detailed logistics of how it happened. It was sudden, and it was shocking. I stepped on Barney. I felt him crunch under my foot.

What I saw and heard is permanently seared in my memory. In fact, tears well up in my eyes as I write this now, so many years later. Barney was immobilized on the floor with his back broken. His head and tail were intact, but he was flattened in the middle where my foot had been. The worst is that he wasn't dead. Hardly. He was frantically squawking in pain as he tried to get up. Recognizing there was no way to help him, my father knelt down and took me in his arms. Safe in the sheltered world of my father's embrace, I buried my face in his shoulder and sobbed just a few feet from our suffering pet while we waited for him to finally die. In those moments it felt like I would cry forever, never reaching the bottom of the well of emotion in which I was drowning.

I didn't go to ballet that day. My father made me change my shoes. In fact, he had me permanently retire them. He made sure I knew it wasn't my fault and took me for an ice cream to soothe my aching heart.

I am grateful for how much Rolf got right in this episode. His quick assessment that there was nothing we could do to help Barney meant the bird's already painful death was not prolonged even further by the futility of heroic measures. He held me in his arms and let me cry as long as I needed to without trying to hush away my sorrow. He remained remarkably present to the situation, exactly as it was, without attempting to deny or fix it. As we sat on the curb outside the ice cream parlor, we talked about the nature of accidents and how shitty it feels to unintentionally cause harm. He took responsibility for having helped create the circumstances in which such an accident was likely to happen. As an experienced bird keeper, he might have known to train Barney to stay off the floor. I could tell you stories in which Rolf showed far less grace as a parent, but in this one he was at his best. I already loved my dad to the moon and back, but sharing this experience with him brought a new level of intimacy and a profound sense of safety.

One of the most powerful things he did was to give me context. He probably didn't realize it as such at the time, but taking me for ice cream and processing what had just happened gave me a framework in which to step back and see the experience through the lens of a greater story, all of which had nothing to do with me—Barney's fondness for feet and that he had been allowed to think the floor was one of his domains, the janky time management that meant trying to do too many things in too short a time, and even the fact that we had birds in the house in the first place. By validating my feelings about my role in Barney's death and, at the same time, creating a larger context, my father gave me the gift of what the great spiritualist Ram Dass calls *witness consciousness.*

In his book *Polishing the Mirror: How to Live from Your Spiritual Heart,* Ram Dass says,

> The witness is your awareness of your own thoughts, feelings, and emotions. Witnessing is like waking up in the morning and then looking in the mirror and noticing yourself—not judging or criticizing, just neutrally observing the quality of being awake. That process of stepping back takes you out of being submerged in your experiences and thoughts and sensory input and into self-awareness.

It is in the ability to witness ourselves that we find a doorway out of the depth of our emotions. How often does it seem like if you start to feel anger, fear, sadness, or *any* uncomfortable emotion that you will lose control? Like if you turn that faucet on, you will never be able to shut it off?

The witness part of yourself exists outside the ocean in which you feel like you're drowning. As Ram Dass points out, your witness doesn't judge or criticize, nor is it in any way attached to the details of your story and what they mean to you. In other words, your witness isn't emotional. Having access to the part of you that exists beyond emotion is useful. I mean, what could be more powerful than that? How many times have I said to myself, if only I didn't feel so much?

An example of what witness consciousness can do for us is my client Anya. In her late forties, Anya is a partner at her midsize law firm in suburban Detroit. She has come to me because in the past many months, her productivity has plummeted. To compensate, she spends far too many hours at work, arriving home most nights after ten o'clock. She stays up late, oversleeps, gets to work late, and the whole cycle begins again. Social by nature, Anya used to look forward to chatting up her colleagues and went to lunch with them a couple of times a week. Now she keeps her office door closed for most of the day and spends many billable hours engaging in online forums and social media.

Anya shows up to our first session five minutes late and irritated. She's lost track of time and is very hard on herself about it. In fact, I notice she is hard on herself about a lot of things. Anya is stuck in a pattern of self-defeating behaviors, which she then beats herself up about, which lowers her self-esteem, which leads to a feeling of hopelessness, which results in self-defeating behaviors. She withdraws further and further from her life and the people in it, as she descends into an emotional rabbit hole.

"Zoë, I don't know what's happened to me. I feel lost and depressed and like I am out of control. I can't get myself to focus on anything that matters. I'm fucking up at work, and my partners are starting to notice," she says.

"When did this all begin?" I ask.

"About six or eight months ago," she replies.

"What was going on in your life around that time?" I prod.

"Ummmm . . . well . . . ."

"Is there something that triggered you? Something that is maybe hard to be with emotionally?"

"Well, yes," she answers. "My ex-husband got married."

"In what way was that difficult for you, Anya?"

"I feel sad about it. I can't believe he is married again, and I haven't had one single successful relationship since the divorce four years ago."

I feel her anger, her frustration, her sadness.

"What are you making this mean about you?" I ask.

"What do you mean, what am I making this mean about me?" she replies defensively. "My husband got married. Isn't that a good reason to be upset?"

I love having these conversations because I know how powerful they can be. The more upset my client gets, the bigger the breakthrough at the other end.

"Yes, for sure, Anya. If you are going to be upset, this is as good a reason as any. Let me put it this way," I explain. "Your ex-husband got re-married. I understand what that means for him. He is a husband, he has a wife, he has moved on from his marriage to you . . . What I am asking you is what his getting married says about you?"

"Oh." She softens. "Well, I think I feel like a failure. The word *loser* comes to mind."

"Okay, good. So about eight months ago, your ex-husband got remarried, and you made it mean that you are a loser."

"Hearing you say it, it sounds ridiculous."

We went on to discuss how Anya's feelings of failure transferred to her work life and how that contributed to her lack of self-esteem and downward spiral. She was also able to see how she has a tendency, in general, to personalize things that have nothing to do with her and how that triggers her into an emotional reaction in which she acts like a toddler (her words, not mine).

After working through Anya's feelings about her divorce and her dating history since, we relieved her of her self-imposed "loser status," both in her personal life and at work. To get a handle on behavioral mood swings, I taught her a simple mindfulness trick to cultivate witness consciousness. Whenever she catches herself either feeling or doing something counterproductive or self-defeating, at that moment of awareness, she pauses and says, "This is Anya having a reaction." Articulating this in the third person immediately removes her from the experience of the emotions and the behavior. She is effectively speaking from the perspective of the witness. From there, she can go on: "This is Anya having a reaction to Michael's email. This is Anya feeling defensive. This is Anya feeling hurt because she feels criticized. This is Anya . . ." and so on, and so on. She has effectively stepped out of her experience into a perspective in which she is an objective observer. From this place of awareness, she sees herself not as a loser, but simply as a person navigating their way through life, having some thoughts and feelings.

Over the months of working together, Anya went on to have some of her highest billing cycles ever, contributing to the growth of the practice. We also worked out accountability so that she stayed off social media while at the office. She also opened her door and invited her colleagues to lunch and on midafternoon walks. I happily attended her wedding two years later.

Owning your shit happens to be one of my personal core values. It's something that I look for in the people close to me. In fact, it's at the crux of the statement "We can meet each other only to the extent that we can meet ourselves." If we are not taking responsibility for our own emotions, we are unintentionally asking our partners to do so. Prior to working with couples on their sexual issues, I always begin with parsing their feelings and figuring out which belong to whom. Matthew and Emily are a good example.

Matthew and Emily had been married for seven years and were dealing with desire discrepancy when he reached out to me for support. He was clearly in distress, and we sorted through what he was feeling.

Matthew rants, "She rejects my requests for sex almost all the time, and it makes me feel like shit. It makes me feel bad about myself. She criticizes me all the time. 'I'm not grounded enough. I'm too impulsive. I drink too much coffee. I eat too much sugar.' She should be appreciating all I do for her and the family. She hasn't had to work a day in her life. I know this makes me sound like an asshole, but . . . no, I can't say it . . ."

"Go ahead, Matthew. Say it; get it out. You can retract it after if you want." I encourage my clients to express whatever it is they are feeling, whether it is valid or justified. It's just one part of the equation anyway. Often the most useful information is revealed in the most outrageous or controversial expressions.

"Okay, it makes me sound like a dick, but . . . is it too much to ask that she wants to take care of my needs by having sex with me? Don't you sometimes just have to take one for the team?"

"While that can be a coercive position to take, there are times when it can be healthy for someone to have sex with their partner in order to care for their partner and to contribute to the well-being of the relationship. Before we work on the nuts and bolts of your and Emily's sexual dynamic, I want to talk a little bit about what's going on with you inside of that dynamic. What I hear is a man who is longing to feel wanted, desired," I reflect back to him. "Do you feel that Emily loves you?"

"That's the crazy thing. I know Emily loves me. I guess I just don't understand how her love doesn't translate into wanting to have sex with me. I am facing the truth right now that I don't want to live the rest of my life feeling like I have to convince her," Matthew replies.

"I am going to make a slight adjustment to something you said earlier. You said that when Emily rejects your request for sex 'it makes you feel bad about yourself.' What happens if you say, 'I feel bad about myself when Emily says no to sex?'" I suggest.

"I am not sure I follow."

"Do you know that great Eleanor Roosevelt quote, 'No one can make you feel inferior without your consent'?"

"I have heard that before. Does that mean, no matter what anyone says about me, I can't let it affect the way I feel?" Matthew asks.

"Not exactly. You can't let it affect the way you feel *about yourself*," I explain. "That's part of it. Someone's inability to see your value is not a reflection of your worth. If someone told us the sky is red, we wouldn't have to think about it. We would simply tell them they are crazy, misinformed, or simply see things differently. But when someone says we are some version of 'not enough,' we tend to believe them, weighing their opinion against our own self-worth."

"I get that, especially if it's someone who isn't important to me or doesn't know me very well. It's a little harder to do when it's my wife," he says.

"Yes, for sure. And it's important to listen to her feedback. It's also important to remember that both of you are perceiving and communicating through the lens of your own experiences—good, bad, and ugly."

"Right. That's where I get confused and react."

"Of course. Welcome to relationships," I continue. "This is the thing with navigating relationships skillfully. We have to remember to take responsibility for our own feelings and to take responsibility for the impact we have on others. These are the two key skills that I am inviting you to explore."

"I think I understand the first one. So, when you tweaked my language around how I feel when Emily doesn't want to have sex, you changed it from 'She makes me feel like shit' to 'I feel like shit.'"

He is getting it. "Exactly. By saying someone makes you feel something gives them all the power. I like to say that we have to *own our shit*. It's subtle, but language is important. Our words are deeply connected to our subconscious. They are the vehicle by which we shape our reality, our world. Taking ownership of your feelings means that you have the power to affect your emotional reaction. It gives you agency."

We continued to talk about tools for taking responsibility for his feelings. For instance, slowing down in general, lengthening the time between Emily's communication and his response. The space created allows him to pause, notice, and process his reaction before he communicates back to her. It's not easy to notice and process in real time at first, but the more intimate we become with ourselves, the more we can recognize and even anticipate our patterns. I also suggested that Matthew step away from a budding conflict before it escalates. It's always okay to simply say, "I am not available for this right now," or "I need to step away and figure out what's going on for me." Before Matthew and Emily can successfully address their issues with physical intimacy in their partnership, Matthew needs to spend some time getting emotionally intimate with himself. Owning his own piece of the equation of their dynamic will free them both to communicate and problem-solve efficiently at the root level.

My father demonstrated this beautifully in the accidental death of Barney. He was clear about what his own feelings were and took responsibility for them, allowing me to be free and clear to process my own feelings without having them confused with his. I can imagine a situation in which a parent is unable to sit with the discomfort of their own feelings when something goes wrong and blame their child as a way of deflecting their own guilt or shame. On the surface it might appear to be the child's fault. At the root, though, the parent is handing the child what I always think of as a big bag of their own shit to deal with. I know well the kind of lasting damage this can cause because I am often unpacking it years later when the child becomes my client. Here's the thing: if there are feelings in the room, someone is going to have to feel them. If we don't feel our own feelings ourselves (own our shit), we are forcing those we are engaged with to feel them for us. This is where it tends to get ugly. Often the person who isn't taking responsibility for their feelings doesn't realize that they are projecting them onto the person they are interacting with, who is confused themselves because they feel as if they are feeling something that isn't really authentically theirs to feel. You can imagine the emotional chaos that ensues when the two people who lack skill try to parse this out. This goes for parents, children, friends, lovers, baristas, and Lyft drivers alike.

The last thing that Rolf did in embodying emotional independence was to *take responsibility for his impact.* He knew intuitively that he shouldn't simply shuttle me off to ballet to distract me from my emotions.

Suggesting that we go get an ice cream cone (his universal cure-all for anything that ails you) was his answer to the question, *What does my daughter need in this moment, and how am I going to show up as the best father I can be?* I am not sure what he had going on that afternoon, but by making my emotional well-being a priority, he took to heart responsibility for the impact he could have on his daughter and adjusted his behavior accordingly.

At first blush this last piece of the emotional independence trifecta might seem contradictory to the idea that each of us needs to take ownership for their own feelings. Aren't we either responsible for our own feelings *or* each other's? Well, the answer is that while we are not responsible for each other's feelings, we must recognize that our words and actions affect others. If I tell the barista that I'm not happy with my latte, I can expect that they receive that information and respond in some kind of way. They might apologize and offer to remake it. They might have a meltdown and feel like they are inadequate. They might get angry and tell me to fuck off. None of these ways is likely to have anything to do with me, personally. Yet as the person who communicated to the barista that the latte they just made is not satisfactory, I have to recognize that I had an impact on them. Now if I choose to express my dissatisfaction by saying, "Hey, barista, you made this latte taste like ass," I can predict a different response than if I say, "I can see how hard you are working, and I hate to be a high-maintenance customer, but my latte is a little off."

My client Shoba came face-to-face with what it means to take responsibility for impact when she started dating Jeanine and they went out to dinner one night and ran into Shoba's ex-husband. Shoba hadn't told Nick that she was involved with someone new. He also had no idea that she had decided to date women. In fact, Shoba had hidden from Nick for many years that she was bisexual. He knew she had had a relationship with a woman before they met, but she told him it was a one-off and that she wasn't attracted to women. Shoba wasn't flat-out lying when she said it. The truth is she was confused. Having grown up in a strict, religious home, she was conflicted about her attraction to women and had been relieved to meet and marry Nick. But now that they were divorced, she decided to explore a relationship with a woman and met Jeanine on a dating website.

The day after their chance meeting, Nick called Shoba. He was hurt and angry that she had not let him know that she was dating again, especially since she took Jeanine to a restaurant they used to frequent together. While Shoba tried to determine in real time whether she had done anything wrong, Nick's anger was focused on the betrayal of not having been forewarned that she had moved on. This made no sense to Shoba since, after all, it was Nick who had ended the marriage more than a year ago. She certainly didn't owe him a status report on her dating life. Finally, at one point during their conversation, Nick said something that revealed to Shoba he had feelings about her dating a woman. Suddenly, it became clear. She understood. For the duration of their marriage, Nick had been insecure about her sexual orientation. She knew that. It had come up many times. Even though she had never done anything to betray Nick, she understood how her own confusion about her history and attraction to women had affected her husband. To be clear, their marriage ended for reasons that had nothing to do with this. In spite of this—or perhaps *because* of it—Shoba was able to take responsibility for her impact on Nick without feeling that she had done anything wrong. She acknowledged that Nick must have felt surprised and hurt and validated that his feelings made sense given the circumstances. Shoba's validation landed powerfully for Nick, and he shared that seeing her with a woman felt like his fears all those years were justified. It made him question everything he understood to be true. They were able to process together and find closure to some of the issues they had dealt with during their marriage that had remained unresolved in their divorce. It was a healing for both of them.

Taking responsibility for impact is a way of listening into the space and crafting our words and actions to optimize the way we relate to others. If we are clumsy or unkind, we are likely to make an impact that requires an additional investment of our time, energy, and emotional labor to clean it up. If we don't clean it up, we leave a trail of unresolved conflict behind us. In practical terms, that looks like anger, resentment, misunderstanding, sarcasm, ambivalence, mixed messages, entanglement—the *opposite* of emotional independence. The way in which we move through the world matters. As they say in backpacking, "Leave only footprints."

Emotional independence is a worthwhile pursuit of overall self-care and well-being, and it's a complex-enough topic to be worthy of its own book. The kind of self-awareness needed for the cultivation of emotional independence is a legitimate form of intimacy and is a significant thread in the fabric of radical intimacy.

EXERCISES FOR CULTIVATING EMOTIONAL INTIMACY

Exercises in which you become more emotionally, physically, and energetically intimate with yourself usually mean that you are allowing yourself to feel more. While this can be a liberating, and often exhilarating, experience, it can also be messy, painful, and disorienting. Before you begin, it's important to conceptualize a safe environment to hold you as you unearth and expose the emotional underpinnings of your thoughts and perceptions. In self-development lingo, this is referred to as creating a container. The boundaries you set between you and the rest of your life (and the people in it) protect you in your vulnerability as you lower your defenses and dismantle your internal coping mechanisms. The stronger the container you create, the more you will be able to let go and dive deep into your inner world. Nota bene: The obstacles you come up against in the process of creating a strong container are often the first indication of what stands in the way of establishing intimacy with yourself to begin with. There are three key areas to consider when creating a container for yourself.

1. Physical Space

Context is everything. When doing deep work that is outside of your normal daily grind, it's powerful to set a context. Creating a dedicated space sends yourself the message that what you are doing is important work, worthy of a legitimate space to do it in. Choose a space that feels good to you. It doesn't need to be fancy or extravagant. It can be a corner of your bedroom or the floor of your candle-lit bathroom. Make it comfortable. Place a few items that remind you of people or places you love. This is your sanctuary; create it as such.

2. Emotional Space

The work you are about to do is deep and foundational. Many of the ideas and feelings you will unearth have been buried for a lifetime. You are likely to have strong emotions come up that you will need to process. It is important not to contaminate the container with someone else's thoughts and opinions that really have nothing to do with you. The gift of this experience is the relationship you build with yourself. After you complete your journey and have some distance, share as freely as you'd like. Until then, if you feel you want support or camaraderie, choose a few friends who know what you are up to, or are even doing their own path of radical intimacy, and speak your language.

3. Mental Space

Most of us never get to the end of our to-do list. There's always more to accomplish, something else to think about, another thing to cross off the list. When you show up to do these exercises, be fully present. Do whatever you have to do to be able to carve out a space with no distractions. Put your devices down, turn off your notifications, and relieve yourself of obligations and responsibilities. This is your time. Give yourself the gift or your full attention.

WITH SELF

Highest High/Lowest Low (Emotional Nuance)

Situate yourself in your sanctuary. Get comfy. Light a candle. Pour your favorite beverage. Think about a time in your life you felt most grateful to be alive—a time when it felt like the universe was on your side, like everything aligned in your favor. Spend some time recalling the details of the experience. How old were you? Where did you live? What was going on in your life at that time? Who were the people surrounding you? Remember how it felt to be you in that moment. When you have brought the experience to life in your imagination . . .

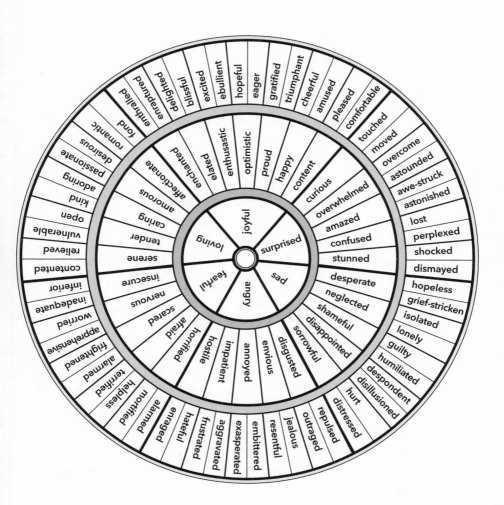

1. Using the Wheel of Emotion on page 73 as a reference, look for at least five emotions you felt during that time.
2. For each emotion that describes what you felt, trace it to the outermost layer of the wheel and trace it back to the core emotions. Explore the range and nuance of these emotions as you uncover the layers of your experiences.
3. Take time and take notes.

The second part of this exercise is likely to be more challenging. Take a moment before you begin, and make sure you have the time and space for tenderness and self-care. Repeat the first part of the exercise but this time working with a low point in your life. If this is the first time you are doing this exercise, there's no need to go to the most painful experience you've ever had. Choose an experience that registers a five or a seven on the emotional Richter scale. When you have recalled the memory of a low point in detail, repeat the three steps above.

You can do this exercise over and over with various experiences in the past—or present. Each time you do it, you'll gain more skill in recognizing and identifying emotional nuance.

Heavy Heart/Happy Feet

What is the physical sensation of feeling emotions in your body? Find a comfortable place to explore. This exercise can be done standing with feet hip distance apart or sitting in a chair with feet on the floor, hands in lap. You can also do it lying down if it's more comfortable for your particular body. Take some deep, cleansing breaths and bring your awareness to your body. It's not necessary to focus on any one part of your body but your physical presence in its entirety.

When you feel relaxed and present, lean into the power of your memory and imagination to conjure the emotions listed on the next page one at a time. For each emotion, explore the answers to the following prompts. Afterward, you might want to journal or jot down some notes about what you discover.

1. Where in your body does the emotion live?
2. What is the physical sensation you feel (tight, warm, buzzing, relaxed, pulling, gnawing)?
3. What is the feeling like (rubber band, melted chocolate, stress ball, lava lamp, carpenter ants)?
4. Does the sensation have a color?
5. Take time and take notes.

Emotions

1. Joy
2. Sorrow
3. Excitement
4. Anticipation
5. Disgust
6. Anger
7. Contentment
8. Doubt
9. Shame
10. Courage

WITH OTHERS

Highest High/Lowest Low (Partner Version)

Discuss your Highest High/Lowest Low with a partner or loved one. Reveal to them the emotions you experienced in all their depth and complexity. Invite them to do the exercise for themselves. Bear witness to them as they share with you what they discover.

The Three Things I Love Most About You

Together with a partner or loved one, name the three things you love most about each other, giving at least one real-life example for each of those three things. Pro tip: The tricky part of this exercise is actually the receiving, not the giving. When your partner loves you up, take it in. Let it land. Imagine the way a warm shower feels first thing in the morning.

Imagine your partner is showering you with love instead of warm water. Can you feel it saturating your scalp and immersing your body?

WITH THE WORLD
Empathy from Micro to Macro
Identify one heartwarming and one heart-wrenching news story.

1. Imagine you are one of the people involved in the story, a stakeholder.
2. How do you feel? How do you feel as a witness to the experience of a fellow human?
3. Can you identify something in you that is affected by this person or people's joy or suffering?
4. Can you feel their experience with them?

Inspired Awe

An acquaintance of mine once defined *awe* as a combination of bliss and terror. *Merriam-Webster* mirrors this by defining *awe* as *an emotion variously combining dread, veneration, and wonder that is inspired by authority or by the sacred or sublime.* It's the feeling of coming face-to-face with something breathtakingly beautiful and not being able to fathom the nature of its existence—where it came from and why. Find a place in nature that you consider to be beautiful—a sunset, a mountain, a forest trail, a beach, a tree, a flower, a body of water . . . Scale doesn't matter. Allow yourself to be fully present, marveling at the magnificence of nature, Mother Earth, the universe. Feel the emotions that are stirred by the experience. Use the Wheel of Emotion to identify and add dimension to what you are feeling.

PART THREE

PHYSICAL INTIMACY

CHAPTER 7

MASTER YOUR INSTRUMENT

PHYSICAL INTIMACY ENCOMPASSES A BROAD RANGE OF EXPERIENCES that include things other than sex. That's a large part of it for sure and what comes to mind for most of us when we think about getting physically intimate. Because our cultural conditions are not favorable for ongoing and open conversation about our bodies' sexual anatomy and physiology, I am taking the opportunity to provide you with some factual information.

Your body is an impeccably designed machine—think Aston Martin or a Rolex Oyster, or maybe even a Stradivarius. Most of us are walking around in these instruments of pleasure without ever having studied the owner's manual, leaving us somewhat unclear—if not completely clueless—about what we actually have "down there" and how it works. Even if you are among the "clueful" ones, I invite you to review and relish these diagrams and discussion of your instrument.

Note: These are drawings used in medical contexts to represent generic cisgender male and female and non-intersex bodies. I acknowledge there are people who do not fully fall into the categories as well as trans individuals whose genitals might be evolving with the support of hormone supplements. Take from these drawings what you identify with and dismiss what doesn't serve.

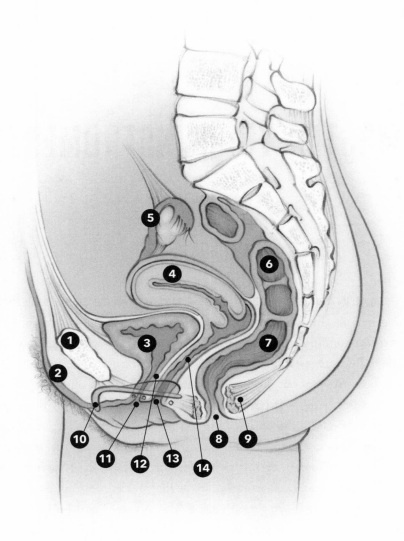

1	Pubic Bone	8	Anus
2	Mons Pubis	9	Sphincter
3	Bladder	10	Clitoris (glans)
4	Uterus	11	Urethra
5	Ovary	12	Skene's Gland
6	Colon	13	Vaginal Opening
7	Rectum	14	Vaginal Canal

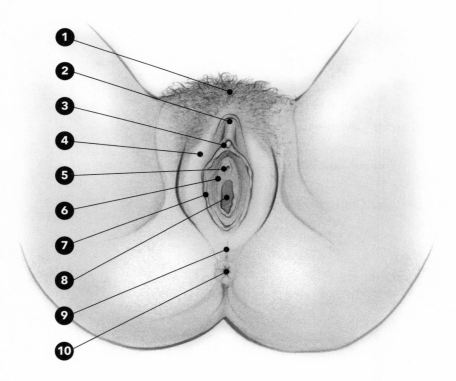

1 Mons Pubis
2 Clitoral Shaft
3 Clitoral Glans
4 Labia Majora
5 Urethral Opening

6 Vestibule
7 Labia Minora
8 Vaginal Opening
9 Perineum
10 Anus

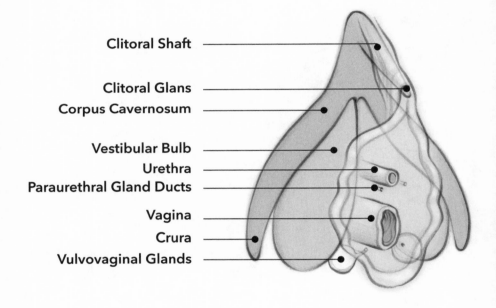

Clitoral Shaft

Clitoral Glans
Corpus Cavernosum

Vestibular Bulb
Urethra
Paraurethral Gland Ducts

Vagina
Crura
Vulvovaginal Glands

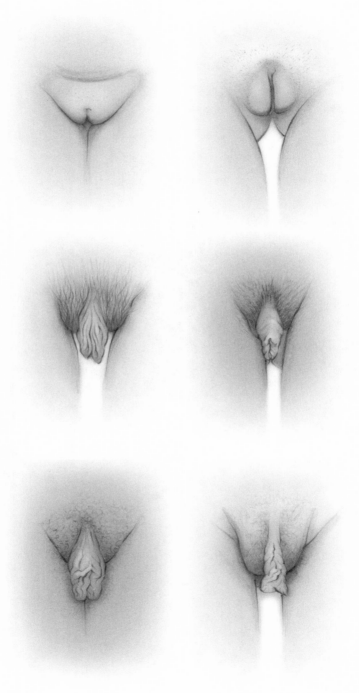

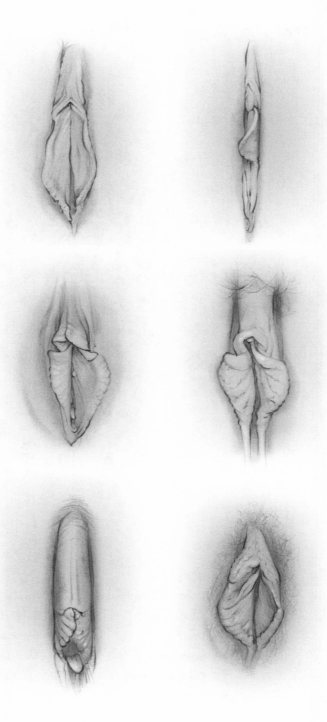

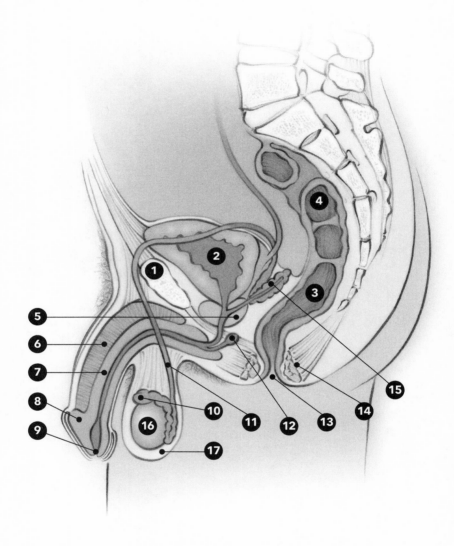

1	Pubic Bone	7	Corpus Spongiosum	13	Anus
2	Bladder	8	Glans	14	Sphincter
3	Rectum	9	Urethra	15	Seminal Vesicle
4	Colon	10	Epididymis	16	Testicle
5	Prostate Gland	11	Ductus Differens	17	Scrotum
6	Corpus Cavernosum	12	Bulbourethral Gland		

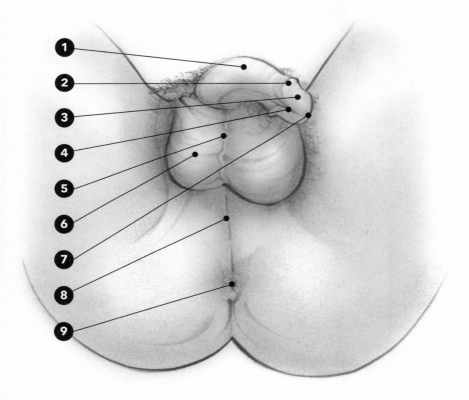

1 Shaft

2 Corona

3 Glans

4 Frenulum

5 Scrotal Raphe

6 Scrotum

7 Urethral Opening

8 Perineum

9 Anus

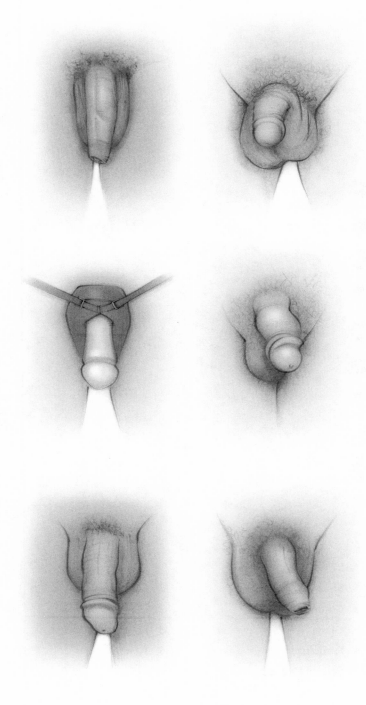

ANATOMY 101
Vulva vs. Vagina

Often, people use the word *vagina* when they really mean vulva. However, the vulva is the word for the entire set of external body parts, encompassing the mons pubis, labia majora, labia minora, clitoris, vestibule, vestibular bulbs, Bartholin's glands, Skene's gland, urethra, and vaginal opening. By contrast, the vagina is the internal muscular tube between the vulva vestibule and the cervix (opening of the uterus).

Vulva Anatomy

Mons Pubis: The mons pubis is a mound of flesh located directly over the pubic bone. It functions as a cushion during intercourse and contains sebaceous glands that secrete pheromones to induce sexual attraction.

Labia Majora: The outer lips that partially or entirely cover the rest of the vulva. The labia majora engorges with blood and appears swollen during sexual arousal.

Labia Minora: The inner lips that encircle the vulva vestibule and clitoris. The labia minora engorges with blood and appears swollen during sexual arousal.

Vulva Vestibule: The area between the labia minora is the vulva vestibule that contains the vaginal and urethral openings. The borders of the vulva vestibule are formed from the edge of the labia minora.

Urethra: The urethra is a tube that carries urine from the bladder to the outside of the body. The urethra opens within the vulva vestibule between the clitoris and the vaginal opening.

Vagina: The vaginal opening is located between the urethral opening and the perineum. The function of the vagina is for sexual intercourse and childbirth. During sexual intercourse, the vagina acts as a reservoir for semen as it travels through the cervix in search of an egg to fertilize. An additional function of the vagina is to carry menstrual blood out of the body.

Clitoris: The clitoris is made up of three parts: *glans clitoris* (the visible part), *corpus cavernosum* (the body), and *crura* (the arms). The corpus cavernous is made of erectile tissue that protrudes to the exterior of the vulva as the glans clitoris. The glans clitoris is innervated by roughly eight thousand nerve endings. The entire clitoris above and below the surface of the vulva becomes erect and engorged with blood during sexual arousal, making it a significant source of pleasure.

Vestibular Bulbs: The vestibular bulbs are two bulbs of erectile tissue that starts close to the underside of the clitoris, splitting to surround the urethra and vaginal opening. During sexual arousal, the vestibular bulbs become engorged with blood, exerting pressure on the glans, corpus cavernosum, and crura of the clitoris. This engorgement of the vestibular bulbs is believed to be a significant source of pleasure in and of itself, but also by the stimulation it causes to the internal structure of the clitoris.

Bartholin's Glands: The Bartholin's glands are two pea-size glands located on either side of the vagina opening. They secrete natural lubricant into the vagina and within the borders of the labia minora to reduce friction during intercourse. This lubricant also serves as a natural moisturizer for the delicate vulvar and vaginal tissues.

Skene's Gland: The Skene's gland is located between the urethra and the bladder beneath the anterior wall of the vagina. The function of the Skene's gland is not fully understood but is believed to secrete an antimicrobial lubricant to the urethra to prevent urinary tract infections, particularly during intercourse. It is the Skene's gland that is believed to be the source of female ejaculation during sexual arousal.

Perineum: The area between the vaginal opening and the anus.

Penis Anatomy

Shaft: Also known as "the body," the shaft is the free part of the penis that stretches between the root and the head. It's composed of three cylinders of erectile tissue: two corpora cavernosa and the corpus spongiosum.

Root: Not visible externally, the root extends into the body, anchoring the penis, and contains erectile tissue.

Corpus Cavernosum: The two cylinders of erectile tissue that sit side by side and run the length of the shaft. It's the engorgement of the corpus cavernosum with blood that causes the shaft to get hard or erect.

Corpus Spongiosum: This third cylinder of erectile tissue in the shaft of the penis encases the urethra, keeping it from becoming occluded when the corpus cavernosa are engorged and the penis is erect.

Glans: Also referred to as "the head," this is the most distal part of the penis. It contains the opening of the urethra through which both urine and semen exit the body.

Urethra: The duct that carries urine out of the body from the bladder. It also conveys semen from the testicles.

Foreskin: The double-layered fold of skin, smooth tissue, and mucous membrane that covers and protects the head of the penis. The foreskin is attached to the glans at birth but by adulthood is generally retractable. The length of the foreskin varies between individuals, sometimes covering the glans completely and sometimes not. The foreskin is sometimes removed in infancy by circumcision.

Frenulum: The highly erogenous band of tissue on the underside of the glans that connects the foreskin to the penis. In penises in which the foreskin has been removed, the frenulum remains intact and sensitive.

Scrotum: Simply put, the ball sac. The scrotum is the pouch of thin skin and smooth muscle located behind the penis. It holds the testicles and along with other parts is essential to reproduction function. The scrotum is located outside the body because it needs to maintain a slightly lower temperature than the rest of the body to facilitate sperm production.

Testicles: Located in the scrotum, the testicles produce and store sperm and are the main source of the hormone testosterone.

Vas Deferens: The duct that conveys sperm from the testicles to the urethra.

Perineum: The area between the scrotum and the anus.

THINGS YOU WANT TO KNOW
Penis Size and Variety

Harvard professor and director of Men's Health Boston Dr. Abraham Morgentaler studied the penis size of 15,521 men aged seventeen to ninety-one from Europe, Asia, Africa, and the United States. He found the average size of an erect penis to be 5.16 inches (13.12 centimeters) and the average flaccid length to be 3.6 inches (9.16 centimeters). The average girth is 4.59 inches (11.66 centimeters) when erect and 3.66 inches (9.31 centimeters) when flaccid.

"What's interesting is, when you look at the curves, you see that most penises actually are fairly similar in size," Dr. Morgentaler says. "You really have to go to the extremes—the top or bottom 5 or 10 percent—to really see some big differences. And truthfully, in my practice, I would say that's exactly right. Most men have penises roughly the same size."

What penises lack across the population in range of size, they make up for in variety of shape. Beyond whether they are circumcised, some penises hang straight down when flaccid; some hang to the left or right. Adding to the range of appearance, scrotums vary just as much. Some are large, descending way below the penis. Some are barely visible.

Erect penises come in a variety of shapes as well. Some curve upward; some are perfectly straight. Some are evenly girthed; some are girthier at the base and taper toward the head. Some stick straight out from the body, and some angle upward, almost touching the abdomen. All of it is normal.

Labia Size and Variety

Because vulvas are hidden unless an individual is spreading their legs, it's nearly impossible to get an accurate frame of reference for the mind-boggling variety of shapes and sizes of labia. Pornography is one of the only places we see exposed vulvas, and the industry has a pervasive habit of showing us vulvas with small labia. The result is the very common misconception that long labia are not normal or desirable. The truth is that each vulva is a unique expression of humanity. Whatever labia you are blessed to have, your vulva is worthy of reverence and pleasure.

Desire vs. Arousal

We often use the words *desire* and *arousal* interchangeably, but they are actually two distinct things. Desire is an urge or hunger for sex. When you see an attractive person walk into the coffee bar and you imagine having sex with them, you're feeling desire. When at the end of a long day, your partner gives you a hug and it feels so good you imagine being naked and melting all the way into them, you're experiencing desire. Arousal is the physical manifestation of sexual response. When your heart beats faster, blood flows to your pelvic region, and your genitals get hard or wet, you are aroused. Another way to look at it: desire originates in the mind and arousal in the body. It's not quite that simple, though. Desire and arousal can occur simultaneously, in any order, and sometimes independent of each other. It's fairly common not to be physically turned on, even though you are mentally turned on. The scientific term for this is *nonconcordance*. Conversely, your body might become aroused even though you don't want to have sex. It can be confusing when your body responds physiologically even though your mind and heart are not on board.

Desire Types

Though it's not nearly as complex as, say, Myers-Briggs personality types, it's helpful to understand that there are two distinct desire types. If you are a Spontaneous Desire type, your appetite for sex is often stirred by simply thinking about sex or by seeing, smelling, or hearing someone or something you find sexy. If you are a Responsive Desire type, your hunger for sex happens when you are engaged in physical stimulation. You will hear someone with responsive desire saying, "Not so fast! I need you to look at me and kiss me a little before we dive in." It's also possible that you are a Mixed Desire type, meaning you experience both spontaneous and responsive desire. However you experience desire is normal and healthy. Knowing your desire type can support you in creating circumstances around sex that will maximize your pleasure and enjoyment.

There are many things that can affect your level of desire. Here is a partial list: stress, fatigue, sleep deprivation, depression, anxiety, exercise, body image, confidence, self-esteem, hormones, pregnancy, childbirth, menopause, pain, medications, beliefs about sex, guilt, shame, relational dynamic, safety, security, cultural conditioning, trauma.

Physiology of Arousal

For people who have a vagina, the first phase of sexual arousal is *excitement*: blood flows to the genitals, causing the vaginal walls to swell, pushing fluid through them that results in natural vaginal lubrication. The labia and clitoris engorge with blood and become swollen and flushed. The top of the vagina expands, and the cervix draws upward, lengthening the vaginal canal, creating a sensation similar to yawning. The pulse quickens as well as the rate of respiration. The blood pressure rises, and the face and neck might appear flushed. In the second phase, *plateau*, the lower third of the vaginal canal reaches its limit of engorgement and becomes firm. The breasts can increase in size as much as 25 percent and appear flushed. Eventually, the glans of the clitoris pulls upward against the pubic bone. During this phase, continuous stimulation is needed to reach the third phase, *orgasm*. The orgasm is the release of the sexual excitement that has built up in the first two phases of arousal. It's characterized by contractions of the vaginal muscles approximately every .08 seconds. During the fourth and final phase of arousal, *resolution*, the body slowly relaxes and returns to its normal pulse and rate of respiration.

For people with a penis, sexual arousal comprises the same four phases. During the first phase, *excitement*, the arteries in the penis fill with blood, causing it to become hard. Rate of respiration increases, overall muscle tension occurs, and the scrotum retracts. During the second phase, *plateau*, the voluntary thrusts of the pelvis suddenly become involuntary and increase in intensity and speed. Body temperature, blood pressure, and heart rate rise. At this time, the penis may release a small amount of seminal fluid or "pre cum," which alters the pH of the urethra so that sperm have a better chance of survival. The third phase, *orgasm*, has two phases. *Emission* is simply the point of no return, when ejaculation is inevitable. *Ejaculation* is when the penile muscle, perineum, and anus contract, propelling the ejaculate fluid or semen from the end of the penis. During the fourth and final phase of arousal, *resolution*, the penis loses its erection and the body slowly relaxes and returns to its normal pulse and rate of respiration.

Pleasure vs. Orgasm

We mistakenly make orgasm to be the goal of sex. In doing so, we rob ourselves of tremendous opportunity for pleasure along the way. I don't mean to minimize the importance of being able to have an orgasm if and when you want to, but the narrative that it's the be all and end all of sexual pleasure is not helpful or accurate. What do I mean by that? We have all had the experience of "chasing" an orgasm. It's that feeling of arousal gradually building, like climbing a mountain. Just as you near the peak, you find that you slide back down the slope and have to start the ascent all over again. Ironically, the more you try to reach orgasm, the less likely it is that you'll get there. By immersing yourself in the experience of pleasure, you get the benefit of squeezing the most joy out of every moment of the journey, but you're also most likely to find yourself tumbling over the edge of ecstasy. People often ask me how to experience the best orgasm of their lives. This is what I tell them: give it to yourself, and don't come for forty-five minutes. We rarely allow ourselves the experience of a prolonged state of full arousal in which our physical reality dissolves into the formlessness of the sexual energy we generate. It is *this* state of ecstatic pleasure that's the real destination of sex. The discharge of that energy in an orgasm is just a bonus.

Clitoral vs. Vaginal Orgasm

In studies of cisgender women, 70 percent of individuals required clitoral stimulation to reach orgasm. Some studies suggest the number might actually be even higher. I am frequently asked by cisgender woman (particularly ones dating cisgender men who watch porn) how to have vaginal orgasms. Many believe something is wrong with them if they require clitoral stimulation to come. Some have even been pressured by their cis male partners to figure out why their penis isn't enough to induce the ecstasy of orgasm. For too many resentful cisgender women and their partners, clitoral stimulation is seen as a chore. In spite of what you have seen, read, and heard, it's an enormous misconception that someone with a vagina should be consistently reaching orgasm by penetration alone. Yes, really. For some, it is possible; for most, it is not. I cannot validate enough the normalcy of the need for (and the great gift of) clitoral stimulation.

The clitoris has long been identified as an epicenter of female sexual pleasure. Roughly the size of a pea, the glans of the clitoris contains approximately eight thousand nerve endings. By comparison, the head of a penis contains a mere four thousand. In humans and other mammals, it develops from an outgrowth in the embryo called the genital tubercle. Initially undifferentiated, the tubercle develops into either a penis or a clitoris depending on the particular cocktail of hormones. Often compared to an iceberg, around 90 percent of the clitoris exists beneath the surface in a sprawling underground queendom. Behind the hooded nub that we see, the body, arms, and bulb of the clitoris create a plump wishbone of nerves and blood vessels that encircle the vagina, with additional arms that reach up to nine centimeters into the pelvis. All of the parts beneath the surface are made of erectile tissue, meaning they swell when aroused, becoming even bigger. This hidden mass, when fully engaged, is juicy with blood flow and crackling nerve endings. Because the clitoris in its entirety is intimately intertwined with the vagina, labia, urethra, and all the surrounding pelvic structures, its impact can be far-reaching and earth shattering.

Clitoral pleasure can sometimes be harder to understand for people who aren't used to providing this type of stimulation. For one thing, studies of cisgender women have shown that even with direct stimulation, it can take their bodies approximately thirty to forty minutes to become fully aroused. That's not to say that you cannot reach orgasm in a significantly shorter amount of time, but the totality of your body's sexual response takes longer than you might realize. Consider giving the clitoris's internal structure the opportunity to become so erect and engorged prior to penetration that by the time a penis or dildo is inside your vagina, it is exerting pressure on your engorged internal clitoral structures. By slowing and extending prepenetrative sexual play, you prime your entire pelvic region for unprecedented levels of pleasure and sensation.

Lubrication

Anything written about sex would be incomplete if it didn't advocate for the destigmatization of the use of lubrication. Anytime one body penetrates another body, it's necessary to add lubrication. It's common practice to use plenty of lubrication when having anal sex. The tissue of the rectum does not self-lubricate, so in order to slide a penis or toy into your ass, you will need to make it slippery. Vaginal lubrication is a natural sexual response. However, the expectation that a vagina should produce enough of its own lubricant for the duration of a session of intercourse is unrealistic and, frankly, misogynistic. While vaginas on the wetter end of the spectrum may not need additional lube, most vaginas would benefit from the kind of loving care that comes from making sure they remain moist and supple. Individuals might prefer all different types of lubes—water based, silicon based, or plain old coconut oil. Respect the vagina you are caring for by giving it the moisture it requires to stay unabraded and tear free. If it's your own vagina you are working with, think of your lube as the most luxurious and reverent gift you can give your precious self. If it's your partner's vagina you are loving, it's important to remember that the degree to which they get naturally wet is not a reflection on you or your sexual prowess. It's also not a reflection of how good they themselves are at sex. Think of the opportunity to lubricate a vagina before you penetrate it like the sacred act of anointing a temple.

Orgasm vs. Ejaculation

The conflation of ejaculation and orgasm is common. However, even for cisgender men, it's possible to have an orgasm without ejaculating. Learning to have an orgasm without ejaculating is difficult and takes patience. Having said that, the heightened awareness of the differentiated mechanisms can provide a richer experience of your own pleasure. Additionally, with practice, it's possible to explore multiple orgasms without a refractory period, saving the ejaculation for the end. If you are interested in learning more about this practice, I suggest exploring the Taoist practice of seminal retention as written about by Mantak Chia in his book *The Multi-orgasmic Man*.

Vaginal Ejaculation

Vaginal ejaculation, also referred to as "squirting," is the forcible expulsion of fluid from the vulva during sex. It can happen simultaneously with or separate from orgasm. Like other facets of female sexuality, there is much debate in the medical and research communities about the nature of female ejaculate fluid and the process by which it is released. If you take it to the Internet, you'll find a vast array of opinions about what is a common and natural sexual response. The source of the ejaculate fluid is the Skene's gland. If you've had experience with yourself or a partner ejaculating, you know that the fluid itself is decidedly not urine. There have been traces of urine found in its composition, which is undoubtedly because it is ejected through the urethra. The fluid itself doesn't smell, taste, or feel like urine, however. It is milky, slick, and odorless and tastes slightly sweet.

For some, ejaculation happens naturally without specifically trying. For some, specific and intentional stimulation of the typical G-spot area is required. Some people describe an overflowing sensation, like when you fill a cup from the faucet until it overflows. And for some it feels more like a series of spurts. If you have a vulva and are curious about your own ability to ejaculate, I recommend using a G-spot stimulator to experiment with various degrees of pressure on the anterior wall of your vagina. If your partner has a vulva, please don't stress them out by your own attachment to making them squirt. It's not something that should be on their bucket list of things to achieve. Let the exploration and experiment be easy and fun.

G-Spot

Named for the German gynecologist Ernst Gräfenberg, who first identified and introduced it in the 1940s, the G-spot has been the topic of ongoing debate about whether it is the source of vaginal orgasms or vaginal ejaculation. In fact, there remains no solid evidence of its actual existence. The location of the G-spot is said to be approximately one to two inches inside the opening on the anterior vaginal wall. Over the decades, anecdotal reports and research have identified in some vaginas a patch of erectile tissue about the size of a small coin that becomes spongy when directly stimulated. Regardless of scientific evidence, many people report the experience of intense pleasure generated from this area. Current speculation has the engorged bulbs of the clitoris meeting just below the surface of the vaginal wall, making it the source of the legendary and erroneously named G-spot orgasm.

Prostate

Often referred to (somewhat problematically) as the "male G-spot," the prostate can be the source of intense pleasure. The prostate is a walnut-size gland located between the bladder and the penis just in front of the rectum. The urethra runs through the center of the prostate, letting urine flow out of the body. The main purpose of the prostate is to secrete fluid that nourishes and protects sperm. If you have a prostate, keeping it healthy is a priority; many people can experience inflammation, swelling, or prostate cancer later in life. Prostate massage can be one of the most pleasurable ways to support prostate health. Though it's possible to indirectly stimulate the prostate through the perineum, it's much more effective to reach it through the front wall of the rectum with either a well-lubricated finger or a toy made especially for prostate massage. Prostate stimulation can be pleasurable for all people with penises regardless of sexual orientation or gender identity.

Aging

We are culturally obsessed with youth in just about every area of our lives. To say that ageism is alive and well and living all over the globe would be an accurate statement. The general belief that the younger we are, the better we are is also played out in our views of sex and sexuality. Nothing could be further from the truth. While it's often true that a penis's refractory period tends to lengthen with age, and hormonal shifts can occur with cessation of menstrual cycles, there are many ways in which sex gets better as we age. My sincere invitation to you is to approach your ever-evolving body with respect and compassion. Resist the temptation to compare the way your body looks and functions to the way it did in the past. There is nothing wrong with the way you are now. Just as you require different kinds of intellectual or emotional nourishment as you make your way through the different phases of your life, so it is with your sexual needs and expression. Stay curious in the laboratory of your sexuality. There are plenty of treasures to discover as long as you are inhabiting your wondrous instrument of pleasure.

CHAPTER 8

THE MIND-BODY DOUBLE HELIX

ONE OF THE THINGS THAT HAS BECOME CRYSTAL CLEAR IN MY YEARS as a sex and intimacy coach is the nearly universal struggle to unwind the internalized messages we receive about sex and our bodies and the emotions that are intertwined with those ideas. Our psychosexual makeup is a double helix (you've seen this structure in a strand of DNA). In order to understand our sexuality, we need to consider each thread. One is the way we think about sex. The other is the way we feel when we have sex. The two are inextricably linked in a symbiotic relationship. To a certain degree, it makes perfect sense that our thoughts affect our physical experience. I'm reminded of how my daughter, Rachel, felt about getting shots when she was a child. She had it in her head that it would be an act of violence against her and reacted appropriately to this idea. When she was eight years old, she even punched a nurse as she approached her with a hypodermic, which resulted in her being restrained by four nurses, one on each limb, to complete the task at hand. No matter how many times we could point to the evidence that not only would she survive an injection, but it wouldn't even hurt, each time she was convinced otherwise. There was nothing in the actual event that was traumatic, or painful. Rather, she was traumatized by the fear induced by the idea of what was going to happen. By the time Rachel was twelve, she was able to successfully shift her narrative about what the experience would be and was able to accept an injection with ease. Her over-the-top defense against the nurse lives on in family legend. And in some sort of act of cosmic justice, she later worked her way through undergrad as a phlebotomist at the local hospital.

The interdependent connection of the mind and body is an ancient and ongoing point of inquiry in the human drive to understand ourselves and our nature. The conversation has existed in the realms of philosophy, religion, science, and medicine since the beginning of time. The range of perspectives and theories about what Descartes defined as "the mind-body problem" is broad and diverse. Even Albert Einstein weighed in, especially later in life when he became more obviously contemplative: "Body and soul are not two different things, but only two different ways of perceiving the same thing. Similarly, physics and psychology are only different attempts to link our experiences together by way of systematic thought."

The mind-body connection cannot be ignored in the pursuit of sexuality, as it is the source of suffering and dysfunction, and therefore potential healing and wellness. How we feel when we are having sex is all tied up in how we think about sex. The challenge is that very often we have no idea how we think about sex because we have been programmed in ways we aren't even aware. In the next chapter, I'll provide a more comprehensive map of your sexual conditioning, but for now, let's look at the mechanics of how this can happen.

Imagine Christopher, a small child, who lives in Vermont. His family's big blue house has a yellow door and sits on a large piece of land with a grassy yard and a stream running through it. Christopher knows that water is

evil. Actually, it's not the water itself that's evil, but the drinking of water that's evil. Or maybe drinking water makes you evil. He isn't quite
sure exactly how it works because his grownups don't like to talk about it,
but he knows that drinking water is bad. Really bad. And if anyone ever
found out that he drank water, or even that he wanted to drink water, they
wouldn't like him or want to be near him. Even worse than that, his parents might not want him anymore, and even God would be mad at him.
He isn't even sure who God is, but the idea of him is kind of scary.

One summer when Christopher is eight years old, he is happily playing
alone in the yard. His mother is inside baking pies, as she does sometimes. It would take all day long, and she has no time for him that day.
Christopher has a vivid imagination and is content to run around with
his imaginary friends, skipping, jumping, tumbling, and climbing trees.
On this particular day, the sun is shining and the temperature peaks at
ninety-four degrees. Christopher is hot. More than that, he is thirsty. His
mouth is dry; his throat is hot. He finds a piece of shade cast by a willow
tree near the stream. He sits for a few moments, looking at the stream,
listening to the water bouncing and bubbling over the rocky riverbed. He
can feel the heat radiating off his skin. He feels tired and a little weak, if
he's honest. He could walk back to the house for some lemonade, but it's
so far away. Besides, his mother is in the kitchen, and she will want him
to help peel apples if he goes in there. He hates peeling apples.

Still sitting under the willow, he closes his eyes. What arises in him
is undeniable. It's a drive so profound, a thirst so deep, he needs to drink
the water. His body is speaking to him loud and clear. He catches himself thinking about satisfying his body's urge, reminding himself not
to get in trouble. Confused, he walks over to the stream and sticks his
feet in. That much he knows is allowed. His body immediately begins to
cool down. Wading now with the water hitting him mid-shin, he bends
over and splashes water on his arms and neck. He is elated. Soon, he finds
himself cupping his hands and bringing water up to his face and letting it
pour down his forehead and cheeks. He is absorbed in the moment, not
a care in the world; he is fully present to the sensation of the cool, fresh

stream water touching his skin. On his fifth or sixth scoop of water, without thinking, he brings his hands to his mouth and slurps down the water. The sensation of his body consuming the water is so deeply satisfying, it could almost be described as ecstatic. Everything about this moment is shouting, "Yes!"

And then he stops. Christopher realizes what he is doing. His mind engages and thoughts flood in. Suddenly, he vomits. All the water he just swallowed comes right back up. He begins to cry. He feels horrible in just about every way possible—physically, mentally, emotionally. He wants to run into his mother's arms, but he can't tell her what happened. He is afraid she will be mad. He is scared of something he cannot even find words for. His heart pounds, and he feels a tense darkness deep in his belly that rises to his chest if he thinks about it too long. The most confusing thing for Christopher is how something that feels so good could be so bad. How could his body thirst for the water in such an undeniable and compelling way if it is the wrong thing to do? Is his body wrong? Is his mother wrong? Is God wrong?

Christopher makes his way back to the house, tells his mom he doesn't feel well, and goes to his room to lie down. He crawls in bed and quickly falls into a deep sleep. By the time he wakes for dinner, his experience that morning is a distant memory. In fact, he won't remember it again until he is sitting in his therapist's office thirty years later, unraveling his inability to consume water without feeling nauseated and ashamed.

By the time he is an adult, Christopher will have decided that drinking water is essentially good and that thirst is a natural physical response to dehydration. Intellectually, he will understand the physiological benefits of staying hydrated. Even so, he will struggle to consistently drink enough water, because when he does, he often has a full-blown anxiety attack in which his heart races, he breaks out in a sweat, and he wants to climb out of his skin, not unlike how he felt that summer day when he drank the stream water. These episodes might even be punctuated by compulsive bouts of secret water drinking, after which he feels the tense darkness in his belly and chest, which he now recognizes as shame.

At the tender age of eight, Christopher was appropriately tuning into and responding to his physical sensations. He found himself caught between two realities: the physical need for water and the idea that it was wrong. The stakes were high: ostracism, abandonment, and exile. The story shows how Christopher was successfully conditioned not to trust his body—a mistrust that got woven right into the fabric of his relationship with himself. If his body is telling him to do something unsafe, then he is by definition not safe in his body. His instincts put him in danger. That's a very precarious place to be psychologically; in fact, it can be categorized as trauma. In fact, he experiences a full-on trauma response when he drinks the water, becoming physically ill and fleeing the scene. His brain represses the memory of the event in an effort to keep him safe from reliving the trauma, a process that might work initially but later results in an aversion and avoidance of the initial trigger, in this case drinking water. Our unprocessed trauma inevitably comes out sideways if not dealt with effectively.

In his widely celebrated book, *The Body Keeps the Score: Brain, Mind, and Body in the Healing of Trauma*, Dr. Bessel van der Kolk says, "Traumatized people chronically feel unsafe inside their bodies: The past is alive in the form of gnawing interior discomfort. Their bodies are constantly bombarded by visceral warning signs, and, in an attempt to control these processes, they often become expert at ignoring their gut feelings and in numbing awareness of what is played out inside. They learn to hide from their selves."

They learn to hide from their selves . . . the very antithesis of intimacy.

In Christopher's story, drinking water is a metaphor for masturbation. I tell the story this way to lessen the chance that you interpret the story through the lens of your own personal sexual conditioning. Because drinking water tends to be a neutral topic, it's easier to see clearly how the mind and body can be at odds with each other and how that can affect physiology. Although we often think of trauma as resulting from an egregious act of harm or violence, it's also essential to consider microtraumas in the pursuit of sexual wellness as a part of radical intimacy.

"We may forget, or be unaware of, how prevalent it is to be sexually traumatized by events that are generally not thought of as traumatizing," says Peter A. Levine, founder of Somatic Experiencing and author of *Waking the Tiger: Healing Trauma.* "Trauma has become so commonplace that most people don't even recognize its presence. It affects everyone. Each of us has had a traumatic experience at some point in our lives, regardless of whether it left us with an obvious case of post-traumatic stress. Because trauma symptoms can remain hidden for years after a triggering event, some of us who have been traumatized are not yet symptomatic."

Ben came to me because he had lost interest in having sex with Kiesha. By many measures, they have a great marriage and he reported that he loves his wife deeply. They had been married for two years, together for a total of almost four. They never had a very active sex life, but according to Kiesha, it was good enough not to be alarmed. For the first few years, they had sex about once a week, and Ben initiated regularly. Kiesha felt from the beginning that their sex lacked connection. The way she put it, she could have been anyone. Shortly after their wedding, Ben's interest in sex took a nose-dive, and she was left feeling lonely and frustrated. Luckily, her high self-esteem afforded her the ability not to take her husband's waning libido as a rejection of her personally, but when she discovered that he was masturbating to porn, her patience and confidence were tested. That's when they reached out. Together we decided that I would work with Ben individually first.

Ben grew up in an extremely religious household outside Atlanta, Georgia. Between Sunday school, youth groups, and the men in his family, he was told explicitly that God wanted him to wait to have sex until he was married and that there was no such thing as casual sex because God unites man and woman through intercourse, both body and soul. He was also taught that masturbation is a sin because it goes against God's intention for sexual expression. He learned that men enjoy sex more than women, that a woman's main source of sexual pleasure comes from satisfying their husband's needs, that the kind of woman who makes a good wife not only remains "pure" until she is married but doesn't have an abundance of her own sexual desire. The implicit message that burrowed deep into Ben's psyche was that sexual desire, pleasure, energy, and expression are tricky and dangerous.

Adding to Ben's increasingly conflicted view of sexuality was the discovery of his father's stash of *Playboy* magazines in the garage. He was fourteen at the time and on the brink of puberty. Simultaneously confused and intrigued, he struggled to make sense of what he was seeing and how they fitted with what he understood to be his family's values. While his head wasn't completely on board, his body responded to the images of dreamy women in alluring poses. It was his first exposure to details of a naked woman's body, and he liked what he saw. There was something stirring deep inside him that he had never felt before and couldn't quite identify. He escaped to the garage to look through the magazines whenever he felt safe enough to do so without being caught. He was careful to leave the stack of magazines exactly how he found them and never said a word to anyone about what he had found. Ben delighted in his secret discovery. He felt alive and energized, as if a part of him was awakened. At the same time, the source of his inspiration was women who he felt sure were not the kind of women that would "make good wives," as his father and pastor described. And, of course, the obvious hypocrisy of his father produced a conflicting swell of thoughts and feelings in young Ben as he was stepping into manhood.

Flash-forward fifteen years, and Ben has long ago left the church he was raised in. Much to his chagrin, he is now struggling to make his wife the object of his desire.

"Zoë, I love Kiesha. We are so good together. She's everything I could ever ask for in a partner," Ben tells me in one of our early sessions.

"I love to hear that, Ben. There's much to be grateful for," I respond.

"I don't know why I can't seem to make love to her the way she deserves," he laments. "And then I have been masturbating instead. I am so confused. I don't want to hurt her."

"It's encouraging to me that you are masturbating. That shows me you have a sex drive."

"Yeah? It's so wrong for me to do that when I have my wife right there ready to go. Why am I so tempted by porn?" He is genuinely troubled by his own behavior.

"I suspect it has something to do with the way you were programmed to think about sex, Ben, not to mention women and marriage. What are you thinking about when you have sex with Kiesha?" I inquire.

"Truth is, I am imagining that we are porn stars. I'm not really there with her, or myself, for that matter." He is less than proud to be admitting this. "I feel awful saying that."

"It's not your fault, Ben, and you're not alone. Many men experience the same thing," I assure him. "Was it different when you were first together?"

"It was. I mean, I was still fantasizing, but I was still really hungry for her. Sometime around the time we were planning the wedding, I noticed I wasn't as interested in sex. But it was a stressful time, and we were often exhausted, so I thought that might be why."

"That makes sense. But now you've found that your desire for her has not returned. Do you have a sense of why that is?" I ask.

"I'm not sure. In many ways I feel closer to her than ever."

"But for you, closeness has never been a driving factor for arousal—in fact, maybe just the opposite," I suggest.

"Oh, wow, yes, that's kind of right. It's almost like, the closer I feel to Kiesha, the less I want to fuck her." He's having an aha moment. "Huh. That's huge."

"What about the shift in desire coinciding with the wedding? What comes up for you around that?" I probe.

Ben tries but comes up empty. "I don't know . . . "

"Tell me about the wedding."

"It was huge. Since Kiesha has a relatively small family, we decided to have it in Atlanta because it would be easier for her family to travel. My old pastor married us. Kiesha had seven bridesmaids and a maid of honor. I had seven groomsmen and a best man. There were more than two hundred guests. The reception was a blast. We had a great band, and everyone danced. Planning the whole thing was one of the most stressful things I've ever experienced, but it was worth it."

"It sounds lovely. Was it rewarding to be surrounded by your friends and family?"

"It was lovely. It was a little weird because I was at home, so I had a lot of people from the church there, and I hadn't seen them in years. My parents had, but after college I never really went back home for any amount of time. It was a little like a flashback," he realizes.

Ben and I went on to talk about stepping back in time and what that felt like for him on an emotional level. We also explored what it meant for the members of his childhood spiritual community to witness his commitment to Kiesha in "holy matrimony."

"It was trippy," Ben says.

"Describe trippy." I am curious—there's something here.

"Trippy . . . these are the people who taught me what marriage is. My parents by example, but also my pastor and the elders and teachers at the church. And then I left them. I didn't really follow their teachings, and I didn't subscribe to their idea of love and sex. But then I went back and got married there. I mean . . . maybe I shouldn't have done it that way. We could have eloped," he laughs.

I laugh with him, but then ask, "Did you feel out of integrity at the time? Did you feel out of step with the expectations of the community that raised you?"

Ben takes this in and clearly is in deep thought. "I think I didn't even think about it. I mean, everyone was so happy for us. Everyone loved Kiesha, I mean, who wouldn't? She's just superlative in every sense," he says, and then he pauses for a long time.

"What's coming up, Ben?" I ask.

"I think I am having trouble seeing Kiesha as my wife and lover at the same time. Does that make sense?"

"It does. Say more."

"I was told that a good wife doesn't want sex and is the picture of purity. But then I also spent my teen years masturbating to women who weren't real. And then I felt guilty about the whole thing. Suddenly, I feel a little immature, and a little messed up." He is a bit surprised and slightly giddy with realization. "I mean, I don't think I ever learned how to truly love a woman. I mean, I love Kiesha deeply, but I mean with my whole heart, body, and soul."

"That's beautiful, Ben." I am moved.

He goes on, "I think I've been playing it safe with masturbating to porn. It's risk free. I don't have to engage with someone else, namely, my wife. I don't want to be fantasizing while I'm supposed to be making love to her. But I don't know how to do it any other way."

"I can help you with that. We need to upgrade your operating system," I say matter-of-factly. "It's going to take some work and considerable patience, but I promise, you can do this. There are two things that are essential to this process, though."

"Anything." It doesn't matter to him that he doesn't even know what he is agreeing to. That's how relieved he is.

"No more porn. It may not be permanent, but it will be a long break."

"No problem!" he says with genuine enthusiasm.

"And also, I want you to understand that you are not broken or bad. You are just a human being navigating his way through life, trying to make sense of all the stories and ideas you've been told about what it means to be a man."

He smiles knowingly, and his eyes well up with tears. "Thank you. I needed to hear that."

"Compassion for yourself will open doorways, both internally, and also in your relationship with Kiesha."

Ben worked hard over the space of a year to deprogram old, internalized beliefs and rewire his brain and body with a new operating system that reflected his current values and devotion to his wife. The bulk of our work was done with Ben individually. I also supported Kiesha one-on-one to heal the trauma of rejection and objectification so that she would be able to stay in the present moment with Ben when he was ready to show up fully. I also did a number of couple sessions to guide them step-by-step in reinventing the way they connect with each other, not just physically but emotionally and energetically as well. Ben and Kiesha worked hard and achieved outstanding results. They now have as rich and passionate a relationship inside the bedroom as they do outside.

In Ben's experience, there is a fairly clear line we can draw between his mind and his body. His own authentic sexual expression inside of his marriage was tangled up with the values and morals with which he had been raised, as well as his father's unknowing collusion in the rejection of those ideas. Often, when a client comes to me, the cause and effect of their experience is not so clear. Suddenly, the double-helix metaphor is simplistic and aspirational as we untangle what feels much more like a bowl of spaghetti. My client Bree was like that—even I was surprised by what was at the root of what she was suffering with.

In her late thirties, Bree was a superstar at her corporate job in Minneapolis. In her spare time, she taught meditation at a yoga studio near her home. Bree was close to her family and had a circle of dear friends with whom she shared many interests, including her dedication to social justice and activism. She organized human rights campaigns and participated in peaceful demonstration on a regular basis. From the outside looking in, Bree lived a vibrant, highly engaged life of purpose and passion. But Bree had a secret.

She initially reached out to me to explore whether she was really giving up on romantic relationships for good. She was happily single and had been for seventeen years. Her last boyfriend had broken her heart when she was twenty-one after a difficult two-year relationship. It sounded to me like he was insecure and controlling. With just a few exceptions in the few years later, she had not had sex since then. At thirty-eight, she wanted to make sure she wasn't missing something she would later regret.

"I am so content to be alone, I can't imagine making room for someone else in my life," Bree says. "Is that normal? I mean, the idea of living with someone and having them in my bed every night makes me feel like I'm suffocating."

"Have you considered having a relationship that includes a lot of room? People arrange their lives in all kinds of ways. Do you have trouble asking for what you want, in general?" I ask.

"No, I am quite confident and have very strong boundaries. I am really my own person. I have my own style and feel really good about myself. I don't subscribe to the popular idea of femininity." Bree goes on, "I think I am afraid to lose all this autonomy. In my one real relationship, I was more concerned for his needs than my own. I am not sure if that's just how it always is, but I don't want to ever feel that way again."

Bree and I went on to talk about her own perception of partnership based on her limited experience, cultural constructs, and societal norms. It was clear that she had a high level of self-awareness and could easily reflect on her thoughts and feelings. The thing she worried about was that there might be some very deep-rooted reasons she felt the way she did about intimacy and would wake up one day in her fifties or sixties and regret never having gotten to the bottom of it. To the best of her knowledge, she hadn't suffered any sort of abuse or trauma that could be informing her choices. We retraced the dynamics of her early relationship—how it affected her at the time and what she might possibly be holding onto all these years later. We did some work around giving herself permission to envision the kind of relationship that would nourish her. We explored what the perfect partner and partnership for her would look like. I had her stand squarely in the perspective of possibility. Bree did this work earnestly. She was enthusiastic about our work and came to our sessions full of energy and willingness. It wasn't until our fifth session that she revealed her secret.

"I have to tell you something, and I am mortified and ashamed," Bree says.

"I understand. I promise you there is nothing you could say that would shock me."

"I am obsessed with the way my vulva looks. I hate it."

"Tell me more," I say in my most comforting voice. I have a great deal of compassion for women who suffer with body shame.

"I don't remember it being like this when I was a child, but sometime around adolescence, my inner lips got really long. They protrude way beyond my outer lips." She struggles to find the words to describe both her vulva and her feelings.

"Bree, that's completely normal and very common," I offer.

"I knooooow. I've looked at hundreds of pictures of vulvas over the years online and in books, and I see that it's normal. But I can't get away from the idea that I am ugly and deformed and that if I am with a guy, he will be disgusted," she says through tears.

"Has anyone ever said anything unkind about the way you look?" I question.

"No! That's the crazy thing," she says. "This is all in my own head. I am so distracted by how long my labia is, I often can't think of anything else. I even walk around in public looking at other women and wondering what theirs look like compared to mine."

"Bree, when did this start?" I ask gently.

"When I was a teenager. But it didn't seem to interfere with my ability to be intimate with my boyfriend. It got worse in my twenties when I would see some of the women naked as they changed in the gym locker room. I started to get very self-conscious," Bree shares.

"Bree, how do you think this plays into your resistance of relationship?"

"I don't know. I'm not sure. I guess I haven't wanted to admit this is a problem, but I am ashamed of my body and ashamed of my shame. It's taken over my life. I'm just a mess."

Bree goes on to describe how when she dated people in the past, she had the mind-set from the start that it wouldn't work out. She says she was always aware of how she dreaded the moment she would have to be naked.

"When that moment would finally arrive, I would be gripped by extreme and excruciating anxiety. My body would totally tense up, and any prospect of pleasure would rapidly disappear. Any potential to participate properly, to really engage with the other person, would vanish as well," she reports.

One experience like this after another caused Bree's anxiety to build and build like blocks of a wall, and, eventually, she avoided the situation completely. She never found the courage to express her insecurities to a boyfriend or partner, or even to a friend. Shame is by nature isolating and self-perpetuating. Bree was a very strong, confident person, and to her this was the biggest failing imaginable. She hated herself for not being able to embrace herself fully, to love herself to her core. She was mortified, as she put it, that she had succumbed to what she considered the shallow and superficial preoccupations of how her body looked.

She says to me, "Zoë, in almost all other aspects of my life, I operate on a very deep level. This is the one area where I can't seem to overcome my insecurities. I despise that."

"Tell me more about your ideas about femininity and the way you embody your personal womanhood." There is a thread I am curious to pull.

"Yeah, well, this is one of the things that drew me to you on social media. I consider myself a feminist, and I am perpetually outraged at the standards society sets for women—how we should look, dress, behave . . . the list goes on. I have personally chosen to rebel against those standards. I have spent many years embracing and loving myself just as I am, without crafting my appearance or behavior to fit the ideas of what's sexy or attractive."

"Bree, how do you think your ideas about femininity and being a woman were shaped by your mother and grandmother—the women who raised you?" I prompt.

"I don't know if I've ever thought about it in this way, but I see that both my mother and my grandmother were expected to get married and have children. Combine that with the church rules about birth control, abortion, and honoring your husband—it's all so violent against women."

"Do you equate femininity with capitulation?"

"Well, I mean, yes, I think I do to some extent. Is that not accurate?" she ponders.

"I don't think there is any one way here. I am curious what femininity means to you and what it is you are rejecting, or rebelling against," I offer.

Over the seven months in which we had weekly sessions, Bree deconstructed the gender trauma of her maternal lineage, that is, the ways in which the women in her family had been wounded by the rules and expectations of the culture in which they were raised. We went back to her great-great-grandmother to understand the limitations of self-expression and self-perception that got carried from generation to generation. This was deeply moving work for Bree. At times she felt anger, outrage, and sorrow. She had moments of profound disorientation, feeling overwhelmed, and grief. There were moments of joy and liberation as well. Bree's real breakthrough happened when we looked at her maternal lineage and the ways in which she had inherited insecurity about her role as a woman, her body, and her sexuality. She suddenly realized that her rebellion against societal pressure on women to meet certain standards of femininity was not so simple. It became clear that her mind had played tricks on her. When Bree opted out of what she called "the popular idea of femininity," she rejected what she perceived to be the manipulation and disempowerment of women—a common and perfectly healthy ideology for a self-proclaimed feminist and social activist. On a deep level, however, Bree applied her beliefs about the systemic vulnerability of women to her own personal relationships. She hid behind the idea that navigating sustained intimacy would require her to give up the personal power she currently experienced as an unpartnered woman. She couldn't imagine a relationship in which her partner's presence wouldn't eventually annoy her, even when I suggested that she might negotiate a relational structure with individual space built in. Behind the facade of feminism, she was deeply insecure about her worth as a woman in the context of a potential intimate partnership with a man. The work she did out in the world to protect women from the vulnerability of navigating a patriarchal society left her unable to be vulnerable with a man in her personal world. The fascinating twist in all of this is the way her mind distorted what was pretty much standard-issue relational anxiety into shame about her body. It was easier to worry about how her vulva looked than to feel the fear of not being enough on a deeper level—which fitted perfectly with her value system that says a woman's aesthetic contribution is superficial and far less important than her mind, heart, and soul. For years, Bree had preventatively rejected herself based on appearance, a superficial wound as compared to being rejected for the totality of who she is as a woman, and ultimately a person.

A couple of months after we completed our sessions, I received an email from her about the results of her hard work. She said, "I recently met someone, and the experience has been beautiful and liberating. After a few dates we had sex, and it was the most incredible sex I have ever had. I truly never thought it would be possible for me to have this type of experience. I was totally immersed in the experience—all feeling, no thinking. My body was alive for the first time ever. It was so deeply nourishing, I came away feeling like an entirely new woman. This work in radical intimacy has taken me on a journey so deep, to a realm of understanding and knowing, that I genuinely feel I have finally, after thirty-eight years, broken the chains that held me down, and quite possibly my ancestors before me too. I now feel totally whole, totally complete, and totally free."

The way Bree thought about sex—the conflation of sex and femininity, her early traumatic relationship, her resistance to sustained intimacy—affected her physical experience of sex. Her inability to feel pleasure and freedom of expression sexually reinforced and deepened her narrative and limiting beliefs about herself. Furthermore, the complexity and craftiness of the mind had Bree's insecurities about her own self-worth as a woman disguised as self-loathing about the way her body looked, which in turn further dampened her experience of and even her willingness to have sex.

For both Ben and Bree, their success in overcoming their personal challenges was a result of their dedication to our two-pronged approach. Each and every one of us has a Mind-Body Double Helix to contend with.

True healing and transformation happens through reorganizing and re-writing the ideas and stories we perpetuate about our sexuality, while simultaneously working with the body to shift the way we experience sensation and pleasure. The metaphor of two strands of the double helix is, perhaps, more accurately replaced by an intricately woven sweater that fits rather like a straitjacket: it looks good and functions to keep us warm, but it's knitted for us with skeins of yarn from all our various influences until we are unaware of the ways in which it restricts us.

CHAPTER 9

SOVEREIGNTY IS YOUR BIRTHRIGHT

For just a few moments, bring your awareness to the heart beating in your chest. Notice the way you perceive its presence. You might feel a pulse in your neck or hear the barely perceptible sound of blood being distributed to your brain. Perhaps you're aware of your heartbeat in other parts of your body depending on the way you have your limbs arranged, the temperature of the room, and how many cups of coffee you've enjoyed today. From the time you were a six-week-old fetus in the womb, until your take your last breath, your heart provides the rhythm of your dynamic existence. You're not alone if you take for granted the workings of this vital organ. Our hearts beat whether we think about it or not. In fact, all of our internal organs do their thing automatically without requiring our attention. We don't need to tell our liver how to excrete bile or our pancreas how to regulate the amount of sugar in our bloodstream. There's no need to manage the way our lungs inhale and exhale. These things are automatic and self-regulating, existing beyond intention, moral evaluation, or judgment.

If our bodies have their own wisdom built right into their operating systems, why is sexuality the source of so much shame? We are taught to mistrust our organic sexual response from the time we are small children. When our digestive system tells us we're hungry, we eat. Yet we learn to ignore, suppress, and pathologize the signals our body sends to our brain when it's hungry for sexual stimulation. Just like every other part of our physiology, sexuality is naturally occurring and healthy. What is *not* naturally occurring is the way we think about it. The way we interpret and judge ourselves and our bodies is learned behavior.

We are born into a context that immediately inserts itself into our self-perception. The context in which we enter the world takes many forms, including the nature of our caregivers and the systems in which they find themselves. Though we are all essentially the same at birth—human infants—as soon as we hit the air, we are categorized, sorted, and assigned identities. It might be easier to separate ourselves from the ideas others impose on us if we were given a memo summarizing the mantle of identity and expression projected onto us, but our conditioning is made possible by the limitations of our cognitive ability. We become the proverbial boiling frog. If you put a frog in a beaker of boiling water, it will immediately recognize the danger and jump out. But if you put that same frog in a beaker of tepid water over a burner, heating it slowly, by the time the frog realizes it's boiling, it's too late to save itself. That the people we depend on for sustaining life exist within the same beaker of boiling water compounds our warped perception. Our ideas about ourselves are created and affirmed by the context in which we are born. So ubiquitous are the things that influence our sexuality, it's nearly impossible to form an organically healthy relationship with this part of ourselves. When we internalize messages as truths, we take the perspective of someone outside of ourselves and adopt it as our own. We do this unconsciously, without even realizing, not only with regards to ourselves but with respect to others as well. Subsequently, these assumptions and projections work their way into our cultural narratives and voilà!—we end up with distortions like the fetishization of Asian and Black women, the desexualization of people with disabilities, and the denial of gender-nonconforming people.

Physical intimacy requires us to remove the filters of influences and have a direct experience of our bodies without the interpretation of the mind. My dear friend Krishna Das says, "You can't think yourself out of a box created by your thoughts." In other words, you need to bring a different consciousness to unlock the juggernaut of mental conditioning. When it comes to sexuality, that wisdom lives in the body.

In working with my clients, one of the very first things I need to understand is how they think about themselves and their sexuality. The discovery process is not just mine. Invariably, we touch on such deeply rooted beliefs and conditioning, they aren't even aware of their existence.

There are six main areas I explore in gaining useful insight into my clients' thoughts, beliefs, and behaviors around sex: Family, Society, Religion, Advertising, Entertainment, and Pornography. As you take in this information, hold what come up for you lightly and sit with it over time. At times, I ask a series of provocative questions that are not necessarily meant to be answered one by one. My intention is more to nudge you in the direction of inquiry and reflection about how you think about your own sexual identity and how you arrived at where you are now. This is deep and potentially disruptive work, and in some respects where the rubber hits the road when it comes to intimacy. As you unravel your own Mind-Body Double Helix, the symbiosis of your cognitive awareness and somatic experience is likely to become more tangible. Move at a pace your nervous system can accommodate, and seek the support of professional help if needed to integrate new information.

FAMILY

Research in the fields of neuroscience and human development has determined the impact of our earliest relationships with our caregivers to be so profound, it affects not only the way our brains function but the way they are formed. When we receive an abundance of tender loving care from the start, both hardware and operating systems are optimized for forming and participating in healthy relationships. We often use the metaphor of a sponge to talk about the way a child absorbs information in their environment. This information can be explicitly or implicitly delivered. For instance, a toddler will learn that a fire is dangerous when their parents explicitly teach them the word *hot* when nearing the burner on the stove. When they get a little older, the same toddler will be explicitly taught that "It's nice to share," or "Everyone makes mistakes." A child implicitly learns by their own experience or by their caregivers' modeling. The classic example of implicit learning is riding a bicycle. The negotiation of body, bike, and gravity is something that is imparted not by instruction but organically by experience. You can explain to someone how to do it, you can give them hacks to try, but ultimately the only way to learn how to ride the bike is to work through it by doing it. Similarly, we learn implicitly how to navigate our world by the experience of doing it. We lean one way and observe the impact it has, then pedal faster and notice how that affects the experience. Through observation and experimentation, we gain self-awareness and relational skills. I can remember reading my mother's mood when I came home from school by the way she held her mouth. I would adjust my behavior accordingly to escape what would likely be her short temper. This is a common relational coping mechanism in a family constellation. On an existential level, our survival requires the stability of our caregivers' well-being. To the extent that they are disregulated either emotionally or physically, they will be unavailable to meet our basic needs. This seems like a simple concept, but it is one of the most common root causes of insecurity and unhealthy relating well into adulthood. Our operating systems are installed early in life by our first relationships with our caregivers. Who they are and how they relate to us, to each other, and themselves have an enormous impact on how we see ourselves and the world in which we live. Consider the messages your parents themselves received and how that might have limited or expanded their capacity to empower you. You are at the end of the long line of conditioning.

The impact of family culture is especially true in the realm of sex and sexuality. Implicit information reaches us through the way in which our caregivers show affection, to us, our siblings, and each other. Think about the difference between parents who demonstrate love and affection for each other, as opposed to parents who don't. If you grew up with parents, or two or more caregivers who were in relationship with each other, consider what they modeled for you. Did they express their love verbally, physically, in gestures, or through gifts? Were you aware of their love for each other at the time? What impact do you think their relationship had on you? It might be interesting to imagine having the opposite kind of experience. How was nudity treated in the home when you were growing up? Were you taught to cover up when others in the family could see you and to what extent? In some families, the caregivers require "modesty" to the point of wearing bathrobes on top of pajamas. Some caregivers create a family culture that includes nudity. What did that teach you about bodies in general, and how did it affect your relationship with your own body? What did your caregivers call your genitals, and how did they speak about them? Were cute euphemisms used to refer to them? Did words like *vulva*, *vagina*, *penis*, and *scrotum* trigger embarrassment? Did that influence your level of comfort with your own genitals? Did you feel free to explore and care for your genitals in the same way you did your feet or your hair?

One of the key areas of your own sexual development in which your caregivers and family members have influence on your sexuality is adolescence. The journey from child to adult is one of the most challenging transitions we make, as humans. A tidal wave of hormones floods our bodies, causing rapid physical, emotional, and cognitive change. It's a time that involves grieving the kid we knew ourselves to be and stepping into the unknown of the adult we are becoming. Unlike a butterfly who builds itself a protective cocoon for its metamorphosis, we get to do it in front of an audience of friends and family. Our tenderness during this time as we navigate our disintegration and regeneration leaves us particularly vulnerable to the interference of others in the formation of our own identity, sexual and otherwise. No time is riper for the internalization of social norms and behavioral expectations as we seek the approval of our community. Think about the way your family created a narrative around your own story of blossoming adulthood. Did the story include explicit or implicit messages about sexual arousal, desire, and pleasure? Were these things considered dangerous, wrong, or shameful when experienced by yourself or others? What about masturbation? The way in which the adults in your life approached these topics were some of your first influences. For many of us, the distinct absence of a conversation sent the loudest message of all.

SOCIETY

Your ideas about sex and sexuality will undoubtedly be different if you grew up in Italy, India, Korea, Mexico, or Mozambique. The age-old aphorism "Context is everything" applies. Our understanding of ourselves and our world is shaped by the particular container in which we exist. First, define the culture you were born into. Where you were born, geographically, is one part of that equation. For example, American is a general category of cultural identification. Specific subcategories of society exist within the broader landscape. Geography, ethnicity, race, gender, and economic status all greatly affect our identities as Americans. It's a different experience to be a Black boy in Brooklyn than it is to be a white girl in Savannah, Georgia. A Filipino girl growing up in Las Vegas has a different experience of herself than a Jewish boy in Chicago. The society you live in reflects back to you your worth, your potential, your expected behavior. It's challenging but important work to look at the systems that define us and accept and reject that influence as needed for our own integrity and well-being. It's also important as members of society to be honest with ourselves about not only how the differences in our experiences shape ourselves as individuals, but also how the system itself is then shaped reflexively over time by the citizens we create.

Society is a self-perpetuating feedback loop in which so many of the assumptions and agreements become ingrained and invisible, existing beneath the surface as if they are innate truths. When viewed through the lens of sexuality, these ingrained and invisible assumptions and agreements become powerful influences on what we think we know about ourselves and each other. Here are some of the common messages we receive from society. See if any of this sounds familiar.

Boys don't cry. Girls are too emotional. Boys just want sex. A girl who has sex lacks self-respect. A woman can enjoy sex only if she is emotionally engaged. Men can't engage emotionally. Women are most attractive when they are teenagers and get consistently less desirable as they age. Men can't get or stay hard when they age. Sexual desire is distracting. Sexual energy is dangerous. The purpose of sex is to create babies. Wives are responsible for satisfying their husbands' sexual needs. If men don't have regular sex, they get blue balls. Women don't need to have sex on a regular basis. Women who enjoy sex are sluts. Men who enjoy sex are studs. Black men have large penises. Asian men have small penises. It takes a long time for a woman to have an orgasm. It's hard to please a woman. Monogamy is the right way to do relationships. It's natural for a man to have his needs met outside the relationship. Women are naturally bisexual. Men who identify as bisexual are actually gay. Men who enjoy receiving anal penetration are gay.

The list goes on and on. None of these things is innately true. They are all contextual. These (and many others) are ideas that have been decided by people who hold the power in the system in which you exist. Excavating the ideas you've internalized as truths puts you in a position to choose the way you define and express yourself to a much greater extent than if you continue to operate from a place of unconscious conditioning.

In his book *Kunyaza: The Secret to Female Pleasure*, my friend and colleague Habeeb Akande writes extensively about the East Africa practice that serves as a great example of what's possible when we entertain alternative ideas about the nature of pleasure and human sexuality. In Rwanda, sexual pleasure for women is considered a basic right. Pleasure-positive sex educators called Ssengas teach young women about their bodies and relationships and encourage them to enjoy sex. They speak with them about consent and agency and also act as relationship counselors and sex therapists. Vaginal ejaculation is part of the cultural narrative. According to Rwandan sexologist Vestine Dusabe, 80–90 percent of cisgender Rwandan women are capable of female ejaculation and do so regularly through the practice of *kunyaza*. To perform this technique, a man externally stimulates his partner's vulva, massaging, stroking, and tapping her labia and clitoris with the glans, or head, of his erect penis. He teases her desire and arousal in this way to maximize her pleasure and ability to ejaculate either before or during orgasm. When his partner is sufficiently lubricated and aroused, he proceeds with penetrating her rhythmically with deep or shallow thrusts (or both) with direct or indirect clitoral stimulation. Alternatively, a woman can use her partner's erect penis to bring herself to orgasm. The inclusion of ejaculation in a Rwandan woman's orgasmic experience is an expectation. The experience, referred to as "pouring rivers" or "joyful waters," is seen as a natural and rightful part of female sexual expression. In fact, Rwandan men are expected to be able to satisfy women sexually and consider the ability to do so a privilege. *Kunyaza* is also practiced in Uganda and Kenya where it is known as *kachabali*. If you are East African or have knowledge of East African culture, you are probably aware of *kunyaza*. If you are not East African, chances are you're noticing some difference between this and your own experience of women's sexuality. What *isn't* different is our physiology. A human brain is a human brain. An East African vulva has the same physiology as a European vulva. A Rwandan penis is the same as a Venezuelan penis. The variable is the cultural context and influence of your specific society. It's worth mentioning that the *kunyaza* technique can easily be practiced with a dildo instead of a penis.

RELIGION

The vast majority of people who come through my door or land in my in-box are reckoning with the influence of their religious upbringing on their sexual expression. For my queer and trans clients, it's not hard to imagine how painfully invalidating it is to be told by the community that is serving as your moral compass that something intrinsic to your nature is offensive and that your organic expression is sinful. No matter your sexual orientation, most have heard the message loud and clear that masturbation and premarital sex are sinful, that the primary reason to have sex is for procreation, that a wife is obligated to submit to her husband's requests for sex but shouldn't indulge her own sexual desire, and that anything that has to do with sexuality is the opposite of godly, divine, or sacred. The simultaneous restriction of sexual activity and birth control reinforces the narrative that sex is precarious for a woman, because they are at the mercy of their husband's desire and potentially thrust into motherhood. It's easy to see how this set of rules and agreements victimizes women and the men who love and respect them as well. Whether these rules are adhered to or not, at the very least they create a dissonance between our bodies and our minds. My clients who speak of the effects of their religious upbringing on their sexuality report that they don't trust their bodies' urges and sensations. They experience conflict between what feels like an innate urge to express themselves sexually and a sense of shame about what they are feeling. They speak of feeling simultaneously right and wrong, turned on and shut down, pleasure and guilt. It takes considerable time and focus to distinguish the source of these conflicting voices and then determine what's authentic to the individual.

I am not here to tell you how to live or what to believe, but simply to invite you to shine a light on the dark corners of your subconscious and come face-to-face with whose voices you're hearing and directions you're following. Whether you were raised Catholic, Christian, Jewish, Mormon, Muslim, or in any other tradition, you have been given a particular narrative about your body and behavior. You have also been given explicit or implicit expectations about your gender role. Religion is one of the most effective and insidious forms of indoctrination because it comes with not only the threat of expulsion from the community but in some cases the wrath of God, or even eternal damnation. Even if you have opted out of your childhood religious context, take a look at where you still feel guilt and shame around the choices you make.

ADVERTISING

English novelist, sociologist, and historian H. G. Wells once said, "Advertising is legalized lying." Companies hire advertising agencies to sell us their products. In order to do so, they need to convince us that we are somehow lacking or broken, and the remedy is found in whatever they are selling. Let's be clear. The success of the advertising industry is predicated on your low self-esteem. We receive a litany of messages that the way we look, smell, taste, feel, and behave is undesirable. We are taught that we are not enough or too much. If shame is the belief that we are so bad or broken that we don't deserve love and belonging, the advertising industry is a shame machine. In a capitalist economy, it's easy to overlook the game that's being played, especially when things start trending and you come down with a good case of FOMO. Especially if you are a woman, think about how you've been marketed to in regard to your body. Now consider how the things you've been told have informed your opinions about beauty and health. Is your skin too dull, too dark, too loose, or too anything? Are long, polished fingernails sexy? Have you been told that your genitals smell unpleasant or that it will if you don't perfume it with special soap or spray? What have you been taught about hair on your arms, legs, and face? What about your pubic hair? Have you been the target of marketing and advertising that assume your sexual orientation? Perhaps you've been explicitly or implicitly told that it's "normal" to be heterosexual. How does it leave you feeling about yourself if you want to cultivate the attraction of someone of the same gender? It's not that any one of these messages has a significant impact. It's the continual constancy of manipulation that distorts our self-perception and interrupts the organic expression of our sexual identities.

It's a powerful point of inquiry to examine the agreements we have made, either passively or intentionally, about how we should think about, care for, and present our bodies. The acceptance and approval of our cultural cohort ensure our survival and on some level are likely instinctual. It's understandable that we want to fit in and be attractive to our peers.

It's one thing when we are talking about the choice between skinny jeans, boot cut, and bell bottoms, but there's a heavy significance to the kind of impact the advertising industry has on us in the realm of the way we relate to ourselves and each other sexually.

ENTERTAINMENT

The entertainment industry covers a broad swath of media, including movies, television, music, theater, and more. So many of the ideas we have about ourselves and each other originate in this arena, it's impossible to even distill or summarize the ways in which we are unconsciously affected by what we see on screens and hear in our earbuds.

Many of the messages we receive through advertising and other marketing avenues are repeated and reinforced here as we observe our idols modeling behaviors we often feel pressured to emulate. Appearance is one of the loudest and clearest messages found in this arena. How many thin white women do we need to see enduring extensive plastic surgery before we start to feel like our naturally aging face is less than desirable? How do you feel when you see your favorite actor's or actress's forehead paralyzed with Botox or cheeks reshaped with fillers and lips plumped with silicone? Do you feel envious, sad, critical? Do you feel pressure to look the way they do because Hollywood holds them up as the pinnacle of attractiveness? Do you worry that you will lose friends, lovers, and opportunities to people who look younger than you?

Gender roles, male vulnerability, and ethnic stereotypes are other significant, and often subliminal, areas of social commentary in the entertainment we consume. A plethora of research has been done on the ways in which the entertainment industry has influenced all areas of society—including social structure, values, and mores—and the ways in which that shapes our individual identities, self-esteem, and behavior. In the pursuit of authenticity and integrity with regards to how you inhabit your physicality and express your sexuality, it is worthwhile to spend some time exploring the ways in which your entertainment choices have informed your thoughts, beliefs, and behaviors.

PORNOGRAPHY

Sex is a taboo topic, and most of us are taught early on that it's not something we talk about. That means we end up learning about sex from pornography in one form or another. If you're old enough, sex education came in the form of your friend's father's *Playboy* magazines. If you came of age in the age of the Internet, you've had a much more robust experience of porn at your fingertips . . . and eyeballs. Vast and complex is the role porn plays in our individual psychosexual development and our ability to relate to each other physically, emotionally, and energetically. The most important piece of the porn puzzle is the misinformation about the way our bodies look and function. Here are the things I find myself saying over and over in my reeducation efforts.

It takes women thirty to forty minutes to become fully aroused. The vast majority of women need clitoral stimulation in order to reach orgasm. Pleasurable penetration requires preparation. The amount a vagina lubricates naturally varies enormously from person to person and from session to session. In order to prevent irritation, most women require supplemental lube from time to time. Spit is not the best lube. Many women don't like to be spit on. Most women are not comfortable putting their legs above their head, and when they do, the angle of your penis likely irritates the opening of their vagina on the posterior edge. Many women are not spontaneously aroused by the site of an erect penis. Most women don't want their male partner to ejaculate in their face. Most women don't sound anything like women in porn, unless they are imitating them. Many women have never experienced multiple orgasms. Many women don't enjoy dirty talk and do not want to be demeaned or verbally degraded during sex. Most women enjoy receiving oral sex when their partner takes their time. There is an enormous range of normal and beautiful appearance when it comes to a woman's vulva, labia, and clitoris. Some women prefer a large penis, and some prefer a smaller penis. The average length of an erect penis is 5.6 inches. Penises don't always stay hard for long periods of time without getting soft periodically. Most men experience nonconcordance from time to time when they want to have sex and their penis isn't on board. Many men enjoy being stimulated in other areas than just their penis, including their neck, shoulders, chest, nipples, groin, scrotum, and buttocks. Many men enjoy anal play and penetration. When a man enjoys anal play, it doesn't necessarily mean he is gay or bisexual. Many heterosexual men enjoy loving, tender, emotionally connected sex. It's not always serious and hot; it's often awkward or funny. Vulnerability is sexy.

I am continually humbled to witness the expressions of recognition, relief, and validation when I debunk the myths that porn perpetuates. There is so much suffering inside of people's relationships with their own bodies and with their partners' bodies. So many people feel broken and inadequate when they don't measure up to the expectations that are delivered through porn. There is nothing inherently damaging about watching people engage in sexual activity. In fact, watching and reading erotica can be healthy, healing, and inspiring. The bottom line is that pornography is a $97 billion global industry. Its primary existence is to generate revenue, not to contribute to our sexual wellness and empowerment.

Sovereignty is a substantive term that is used in political theory to define a nation or state's ultimate authority over its own governance and maintenance of order. When an entity is sovereign, it is independently regulated and free from external control. There are certain things due to you by nature of being born into a human body. One of them is your absolute and inviolable authority over your own governance. In the world we want to create, you have the right to define and embody your physicality, particularly your sexual expression, in any way you want—your body, your life, your rules. No one gets to tell you what you should want, how you should feel, or who you should be. This life is yours to create for yourself. Choose your influences and inspiration consciously and intentionally. Your choices and decisions should be free from external control. You do you. Then encourage everyone else to do the same.

EXERCISES FOR CULTIVATING PHYSICAL INTIMACY

The exercises herein are designed to support you in having a direct experience with your body. Often without realizing it, we experience our physicality through the filter of our busy mind. By the time we sense something physically, we recognize the feeling through the interpretation and judgment of the thoughts, ideas, and beliefs that are rooted in our conditioning. My invitation to you is this: Allow yourself the opportunity to step out of your normal mind-set of right and wrong, good and bad, should or shouldn't. Adopt an attitude of curiosity and unconditional positive regard for this body you inhabit. Open up to the possibility that you might discover something new—about yourself, about your body, about the amount and kind of sensation you are able to feel. Treat these exercises as if you are stepping into a laboratory in which you explore the limits and capabilities of your instrument. Approach your experimentation as a fact-finding mission. You are simply learning and playing with what is so. For some, it may not feel empowering to become more familiar with your genitals. This could be due to sexual trauma, gender distress, or other circumstances specific to you. I've included a version of self-pleasure without genital stimulation. If you are a person with a disability that makes these exercises uncomfortable or impossible to execute, I invite you to adapt them or eliminate them as needed. They are suggestions, not requirements.

WITH SELF
Mirror Exercise

For so many of us, the anticipation of getting naked in front of a partner is the source of great anxiety and self-doubt. Seeing ourselves naked can be equally crushing when we don't like what we see in the mirror. We can be so hard on ourselves—the things we so easily find beautiful and alluring in others are often the basis of self-loathing and ridicule. How many times have you averted your eyes from the mirror while getting undressed, so you're not confronted by the reality of how your body looks?

Feeling confident and comfortable in your skin means you are more available for connection and intimacy because you are not distracted by worries about not being enough. Growing your body self-esteem takes both time and intention. The appreciation of your body as a miraculous, sexy instrument of pleasure is a gift that only you can give yourself. Doing this exercise in earnest consistently will help you unravel the conditioning you've received about how you think you *should* look and cultivate a deep love and appreciation of how you do you.

I suggest getting yourself a special journal or notebook to keep a running log of this exercise. It might be helpful to notice how your entries change over time.

- Take a few moments to be still and quiet.
- Close your eyes and imagine that you live in a society in which your physical form was celebrated as beautiful and desirable.
- Stand or sit in front of a full-length mirror as close to naked as you can tolerate.
- Write down in your journal everything you see that you like.
- Pick one physical attribute to focus on. Write a few words about what you appreciate about that body part. What is beautiful about it? What has its function afforded you all these years? What is its superpower? Why are you grateful for it?
- Repeat daily.

Note: This exercise is particularly powerful for embracing parts of your body that trigger shame. It's tender work, and you might keep a box of tissues nearby, but stick with it. No matter what you wish you look like, or what comparisons you make, your body is beautiful and perfect exactly as it is. Most of all, it's *yours*. Identify and, as hard as it might be, put aside the cultural context of all the internalized messages and see yourself through the lens of love and admiration. If you struggle to find things about your body you like, start small. You might find the pleasing shape of one of your toenails or a particularly lovely patch of skin on the inside of your elbow. Even the smallest amount of love you are able to give yourself can be powerful and can expand over time.

Bathe Mindfully

Note: If you don't have a tub or bathing isn't doable for your body, a foot or hand bath can create the same kind of sensation. You might also look at the Mindful Showering practice on page 211.

Draw a bath for yourself, paying attention to the temperature of the water so that it feels soothing. Create an environment that both stimulates your senses and relaxes your mind and body. Candlelight, bath oil, flowers, your favorite playlist . . . whatever it takes to help you feel safe and held. You will need a washcloth, sponge or loofah, and some liquid soap.

Standing by the side of your bathtub, take a moment to land. Present yourself in the environment by taking in the scene. Notice the quality of light, the temperature of the air on your skin, the smells, sounds, and feel of the room. Bring your awareness to your thoughts, emotions, and the physical sensations of your body without judgment. Simply notice what is happening internally and externally.

Step slowly into the tub. Notice the feeling of your body as it meets the water. How does the wetness feel on your foot? What does the disturbance of the water look like, sound like? Stand with both feet in the water for a moment. As you lower the rest of your body into the water, bring your awareness to the sensation of immersion.

And now settle into a comfortable position, either sitting or reclining with as much of your body submerged as possible. Notice again the way the disturbance of the water looks, sounds, and feels as you arrange your body.

Lying still for a few moments, bring your awareness to the physical sensation of your breath. Notice the feeling of the air traveling in through your nostrils, past your throat, and into your lungs. Observe the same as you slowly exhale.

Wiggle your toes and your fingers, and allow your arms to float to the surface of the water. What do you hear, see, smell, feel? Spend a few minutes here. As thoughts drift in, notice them without judgment. Don't try to clear your mind; simply allow the thoughts to pass through as you gently bring your awareness back to the internal and external sensations of your environment. Just simply be here now.

And now, if you are reclining, sit up and locate your washcloth or sponge and soap. Squeeze a generous amount of soap on your scrubbing device and lather it up. Move slowly and deliberately as you gently wash your body. Start with your forearms, upper arms, under arms, shoulders, neck, and chest. Notice the different sensations of the cloth or sponge on your skin, the slickness of the soap, the different sensations of different body parts, the sensation of your lower body as it's still submerged.

When you are ready, rinse the soap off your body by cupping your hands to carry water over your body. You can also splash water over your upper body. Take this opportunity to create more sensations to observe. What is the sound of the water splashing? How does it feel to scoop water into your hands? You may also want to submerge your body as much as possible to rinse off the remaining suds.

When you are ready, slowly and carefully get out of the bath and grab a towel. As you dry yourself off, think about what you appreciate about your body, not just how it looks, but how it functions. Are there parts of your body that give you a sense of pleasure or pride? Are there any parts of your body that you do not appreciate? Your body is alive. Are there aspects of your body that deserve more attention? As you do this, notice how you feel now as compared to before your bath. What has shifted? What has remained the same? As you complete this exercise, do your best to find loving awareness and acceptance of the extraordinariness of your body. Thank yourself for the gift of this mindful bathing exercise.

Shift Your Self-Pleasure Script

So often, we make orgasm the focus and purpose of sex. The same is true with masturbation. While there is much to be said about the joys and benefits of reaching orgasm, by making it the goal, we miss an incredible opportunity to experience pleasure along the way. When Ralph Waldo Emerson said, "The journey is the destination," he wasn't talking about masturbation, but he might as well have been. In this exercise, I invite you to slow down and explore, experience, and enjoy your body as you never have before.

Begin by setting the stage. Create a sexy atmosphere in which to explore and honor your body. Assemble some pillows and blankets on the floor or bed. Light some candles. Play some meditative or erotic music. Dim the lights. Make sure to have a small dish or jar of coconut oil or other genital-safe lubricant within reach. You will be lubricating as needed throughout. This exercise is most effectively done without clothes.

For People with a Vulva

Begin by taking a small amount of oil with your dominant hand and placing your fingers on the palm of your other hand. Start to slowly move the flat part of your fingertips in a circular motion against your palm. Take your forefinger and middle finger and trace the lines on your palm. Notice how this feels. Bring your awareness to the sensation in your palm. Continue using your fingertips to explore the fingers on your other hand. Run your forefinger along the ridge where your hand joins your fingers, feeling the skin between your fingers. Gently trace each finger, noticing the different sensations as your fingertip touches the creases where your joints are and the flesh in between. Make your way to the base of your thumb and the heel of your hand. Return to circular motions as you caress this part of your hand.

Lubricate as needed to keep your fingers comfortably moving across your skin. Extend your touch to the inside of your wrist, lingering at the joint where your hand joins your arm. Notice the sensation. Caressing your whole inner forearm, vary your touch from a very light tickle to a firm massage stroke and back again. Feeling all the sensations there are to feel, move to your upper arm, shoulder, and underarm. Spend some time here, revisiting your elbow and forearm as well.

On your next pass over your shoulder and upper arm, reach around to the side of your chest. Your arm will be crossing your body at this point. Circle your chest with the palm of your hand, paying close attention to the sensation as your hand touches the ribs. Linger there for a few moments, massaging this area. Continue to your breastbone, or sternum. Explore this area, feeling for where your breastbone ends at the bottom of your heart and follow it up to your collarbone, or clavicle. Continuing to circle your chest, reach your hand back toward your shoulder. With your hand flat against your skin, circle the chest, this time exploring your nipple. Notice all the sensation . . . all the feeling. Spend a few moments here. Breathe deeply. Let out a sigh on your next exhale.

Grabbing some more oil, explore both your chest and nipples with both your hands. Be playful. Be curious. There is no right or wrong way to do this. Let your body guide you to touch it in the way it wants to be touched. How long does it want your strokes to be? How hard or soft? How fast or slow? Do your nipples want to be squeezed or tugged?

Lubricating as needed, now bring your hands to your abdomen. Explore the way your ribs part, giving way to the softness of your belly. This is one of the most vulnerable places on your body. How do you feel when you are stimulating this part of your body? Place one hand on your upper abdomen above your navel and one hand on your lower abdomen below your navel. Take a deep breath all the way down into the deepest part of your belly. Notice your body pushing against the palms of your hands. On the exhale, press your hands against your skin and begin to massage and caress the front side of your torso in its entirety.

Bring your attention to your pelvis. Notice, as your hand glides over your hip bones, how your flesh rises and falls. Now let your hands explore the place where your pubic bone meets your lower abdomen. Imagine this as the threshold to your genitals. Let your fingers dance around this area . . . curious and eager . . . awakening your arousal. Notice the sensations stimulated by your touch. And notice the sensations elsewhere in your body. What do you feel in your chest as you breathe? What sensations are happening in your neck and head? What do you notice happening in your vagina?

Now slide your well-lubricated hands to the crease where your hips meet your thighs. Run your fingers from the outside of your legs toward your groin as you gently spread your legs. Placing your nondominant hand on your lower abdomen, use your dominant hand to explore the very top of your inner thighs, where your groin meets the very outer lips of your vulva. Spend a few moments here, noticing all the sensations and the growing hunger of your vulva to be touched.

Now, finally, slip a finger or two over your outer lips and find your inner lips, your labia minora. Add lubrication if needed so that your fingers slip in and out of all the folds. Caress and stroke them. Imagine that you are discovering the most beautiful place you've ever seen. Every nuance is more magical than the next. Avoiding your clitoris for now, spend some time here exploring your labia.

Now without making direct contact, take your forefinger or your middle finger and trace a wide circle around your clitoris. Continue to circle around, varying the strength of your touch. Notice the different sensations and what feels good. Allow your finger to run over the upper hood of your clitoris. There are many nerve endings here. Move slowly to increase the sensation.

Take the flat part of one fingertip and begin to lightly tap your clitoris directly—at a slow pace of about one tap per second. Notice what happens in the space between taps. Is your level of arousal increasing? Are you craving more touch? Allow the desire to build and expand.

Now run your fingers around your labia again, revisiting all the sensations available to you in your petals. As you explore, slip one or two fingers into the opening of your vagina. Notice any pulsations or contractions as your vagina craves more.

Use both hands to explore, massage, and stimulate all parts of your vulva now, including your clitoris and your vagina, to the extent that you can reach. As you get close to orgasm, resist. Pull your hands away and breathe. Imagine you are circulating the electric energy throughout your body.

Continue to self-pleasure, edging toward orgasm and backing away. This increases your capacity to feel sensation and hold energy. Cycle through this sequence two or three more times. When you are ready to come, bring all your awareness to the energetic sensation happening in your body. Allow your expression through your voice or emotions (laughter, tears, and so on). Be present to the experience of your whole body.

In the afterglow, take some deep breaths and thank yourself for the gift of pleasure.

For People with a Penis

Begin by taking a small amount of oil with your dominant hand and placing your fingers on the palm of your other hand. Start to slowly move the flat part of your fingertips in a circular motion against your palm. Take your forefinger and middle finger and trace the lines on your palm. Notice how this feels. Bring your awareness to the sensation in your palm. Continue using your fingertips to explore the fingers on your other hand. Run your forefinger along the ridge where your hand joins your fingers, feeling the skin between your fingers. Gently trace each finger, noticing the different sensations as your fingertip touches the creases where your joints are and the flesh in between. Make your way to the base of your thumb and the heel of your hand. Return to circular motions as you caress this part of your hand.

Lubricate as needed to keep your fingers comfortably moving across your skin. Extend your touch to the inside of your wrist, lingering at the joint where your hand joins your arm. Notice the sensation. Caressing your whole inner forearm, vary your touch from a very light tickle to a firm massage stroke and back again. Feeling all the sensations there are to feel, move to your upper arm, shoulder, and underarm. Trace the shape of your muscles and tendons below your skin, alternating between using your fingertips and your whole palm, flat against your skin. Spend some time here, revisiting your elbow and forearm as well.

On your next pass over your shoulder and upper arm, reach around to the side of your chest. Your arm will be crossing your body at this point. Circle your chest with the palm of your hand, paying close attention to the sensation as your hand touches the ribs under your muscle. Linger there for a few moments, massaging this area. Continue around your chest to your sternum, or breastbone. Explore this area, feeling for where your breastbone ends at the bottom of your heart and follow it up to your collarbone, or clavicle. Continuing to circle your pectoral muscle, reach your hand across your chest above your pec and back toward your shoulder. With your fingertips, now include your nipple. Notice all the sensation . . . all the feeling.

Spend a few moments here. Breathe deeply. Let out a sigh on your next exhale. Grabbing some more oil, explore your whole chest with both your hands. Be playful. Be curious. There is no right or wrong way to do this. Let your body guide you to touch it in the way it wants to be touched. How long does it want your strokes to be? How hard or soft? How fast or slow? Do your nipples want to be squeezed or rubbed?

Lubricating as needed, now bring your hands to your abdomen. Explore the way your ribs part, giving way to your belly. This is one of the most vulnerable places on your body. How do you feel when you are stimulating this part of your body? Place one hand on your upper abdomen above your navel and one hand on your lower abdomen below your navel. Take a deep breath all the way down into the deepest part of your belly. Notice your body pushing against the palms of your hands. On the exhale, press your hands against your skin and begin to massage and caress the front side of your torso in its entirety.

Let your hands wander down to your thighs. Run your flat hands down the tops of your thighs and around and up your outer thighs. Circle around your hips and back down the tops of your thighs. Stay with this circular motion for a while, varying the pressure of your touch. Notice all the sensations.

Add oil as needed to keep your hands moving freely across your skin. Now as your hands circle your hips next time, let your hands move to your groin. Avoiding your penis for now, keep your hands flat on your inner thighs and massage. You might spread your legs as needed for comfort and reach. Play with the intensity of your touch, from actually squeezing your inner thigh to a light tickle, and back again.

Moving your fingers to your groin, massage the area where your scrotum meets your groin. Explore different types of touch here. Gradually include more and more of your scrotum, moving your penis aside if necessary. Make sure to reach down and massage your perineum, or taint. In doing so, you might also massage your anus.

And now it's finally time to include your penis. If you are erect, begin stroking at the base of your penis with a firm short stroke. Spend some time here, exploring the sensation of the base of your shaft as it extends into your body below the surface. Keeping your pace very slow, gradually increase the length of your stroke. Take your time. Each stroke should be just a little bit longer, letting your hand move closer and closer to the head of your penis. Adding plenty of lubricant, move your hand with long, slow strokes from the base of your penis all the way to the tip. As you reach the head, circle your hand around the head, stimulating the glans on the underside of the tip of your penis. Feel the difference in sensation at the base of your penis, the shaft, and the head.

Shorten your stroke now, concentrating on the tip of your penis. Don't let your hand go all the way back to the base. As you vary the speed and pressure on the head, use the edge of your forefinger to add extra stimulation to the glans of your penis, that sensitive spot on the underside of the head. Slow way down for a few moments, lingering on that spot. Feel the sensation radiating from that spot. How far does the pleasure sensation go? What does it feel like exactly? Notice that.

Continue to stroke your penis with one hand while exploring your scrotum and perineum with the other. Take your testicles in your hand and lightly massage. Gently tug on your scrotum, pulling it away from your body, again noticing how that feels. You might reach all the way down to your perineum and massage with your fingertips. Alternatively, you might use your other hand to massage your abdomen or chest.

Keep stroking your penis, varying the length, strength, and position of your stroke. As your arousal heightens and you near orgasm, back off and focus on your breath. Edging toward climax and backing off builds the sensation in your body and increases your capacity to hold sexual energy. Feel that. Feel the energy circulating through your whole body. Play with this edge for a while until you finally allow the pleasure to spill over into orgasm.

Self-Pleasure Without Genital Stimulation

Begin by taking a small amount of oil with your dominant hand and placing your fingers on the palm of your other hand. Start to slowly move the flat part of your fingertips in a circular motion against your palm. Take your forefinger and middle finger and trace the lines on your palm. Notice how this feels. Bring your awareness to the sensation in your palm. Continue using your fingertips to explore the fingers on your other hand. Run your forefinger along the ridge where your hand joins your fingers, feeling the skin between your fingers. Gently trace each finger, noticing the different sensations as your fingertip touches the creases where your joints are and the flesh in between. Make your way to the base of your thumb and the heel of your hand. Return to circular motions as you caress this part of your hand.

Lubricate as needed to keep your fingers comfortably moving across your skin. Extend your touch to the inside of your wrist, lingering at the joint where your hand joins your arm. Notice the sensation. Caressing your whole inner forearm, vary your touch from a very light tickle to a firm massage stroke and back again. Feeling all the sensations there are to feel, move to your upper arm, shoulder, and underarm. Spend some time here, revisiting your elbow and forearm as well.

On your next pass over your shoulder and upper arm, reach around to the side of your chest. Your arm will be crossing your body at this point. Drag your hand across your torso and spend a few moments massaging your chest.

Continue to the very center of your chest. This is your breastbone, or sternum. Explore this area, feeling for where your breastbone ends at the bottom of your heart and follow it up to your collarbone, or clavicle.

Continuing to circle your chest, reach your hand across your chest and back toward your shoulder. With your hand flat against your skin, circle your chest again, this time exploring your nipple. Notice all the sensation . . . all the feeling. Spend a few moments here. Breathe deeply. Let out a sigh on your next exhale.

Grabbing some more oil, explore both your nipples with both your hands. Be playful. Be curious. There is no right or wrong way to do this. Let your body guide you to touch it in the way it wants to be touched. How long does it want your strokes to be? How hard or soft? How fast or slow? Do your nipples want to be squeezed or tugged?

Lubricating as needed, now bring your hands to your abdomen. Explore the way your ribs part, giving way to the softness of your belly. This is one of the most vulnerable places on your body. How do you feel when you are stimulating this part of your body? Place one hand on your upper abdomen above your navel and one hand on your lower abdomen below your navel. Take a deep breath all the way down into the deepest part of your belly. Notice your body pushing against the palms of your hands. On the exhale, press your hands against your skin and begin to massage and caress the front side of your torso in its entirety.

Bring your attention to your pelvis. Notice, as your hand glides over your hip bones, how your flesh rises and falls. Now let your hands explore the place where your pubic bone meets your lower abdomen. Let your fingers dance around this area, awakening your arousal. Notice the sensations stimulated by your touch. And notice the sensations elsewhere in your body. What do you feel in your chest as you breathe? What sensations are happening in your neck and head? What do you notice happening in your pelvic region?

From here, you might continue to explore in a way that feels good, staying in the experience of sensual touch that may or may not lead to orgasm. If you are ready to complete the exercise, place one hand palm down on your lower abdomen and one on your chest over your heart. Take some deep breaths and circulate the energy you feel throughout your body. If intrusive thoughts or judgments arise, let them float through without indulging them, turning your attention back to your precious body and the pleasurable sensation it can generate.

WITH OTHERS

Wholly Giving, Wholly Receiving

In a world in which sex is often regarded as transactional (I'll do this for you, and then you do this for me . . .), it can be a great source of healing for one partner to wholly give and one to wholly receive. The following guided exercise is designed to support you in creating a space in which your partner can surrender completely to the experience of receiving. I recommend doing this on separate occasions, alternating who plays which role: giver and receiver.

Find a comfortable space on the floor for your partner to lie down. They should be wearing loose, comfortable clothing. Use blankets and pillows to support their body and relieve pressure on joints and muscles as needed. Create a soothing atmosphere with soft music and dim lighting. The temperature of the room should be comfortably warm. If it is too cool, have a blanket ready to cover your partner if needed.

Once your partner is comfortably situated, you're ready to go.

Begin by sitting behind your partner's head and placing your hands palm down on their shoulders. You want your touch to be gentle but firm. This means that your hands are confidently placed with a medium to light amount of pressure. Simply keep your hands there while you take three deep breaths.

Now slowly begin to lift your hands and slide them slowly around to the outside of the shoulders and stop. Apply light pressure as each hand holds a shoulder. Pause long enough for one deep inhalation and exhalation.

Slowly release your hands from their shoulders and begin to run your fingers through their hair. Use the very tips of your fingers and your fingernails. If your partner is bald, continue to use the whole palms of your hands as you did on their shoulders. Continue this for a full two minutes.

Place the palm of one hand on your partner's forehead. Apply gentle pressure. Stay here while you take two deep breaths. The next phase of this exercise requires you to move around your partner. You may maneuver around on your knees or stand on your feet and walk around.

You are going to use your two hands to apply pressure to various parts of their body. In doing so, you will be using nonsexual touch to calm their nervous system and instill a feeling of safety and a state of deep relaxation. You will do this through their clothes or blanket if there is one.

Remove your hand from your partner's forehead and move to their feet. Kneel down so that the soles of your partner's feet are resting on your knees. Place one hand on the top of each foot and gently squeeze. Stay here for a moment. Release and reapply pressure once or twice.

Release the feet and move to your partner's side near their knees. Place one palm on each of their thighs, midway between their knees and hips, keeping your hands flat against their quadriceps muscles. Take a deep inhalation, and as you exhale slowly, gently press your palms into their thighs. Take another deep, long breath here, and as you exhale, rock your hands side to side. Imagine you are gently pressing any tension in your partner's muscles with your hands. Imagine they are melting under your touch. Release the pressure and still your hands. Take one more deep breath, and as you exhale this time apply gentle smooth pressure, not rocking your hands but keeping them still and steady. Stay here for a few moments.

Now remove your hands from your partner's thighs and place them on their hip bones. Repeat this sequence of three deep breaths while you apply pressure to your partner's hips as you exhale.

As you continue, bring to your energy the intention to give wholly as they receive. Imagine you are infusing your touch with warm, loving energy.

Next place one hand on your partner's heart. Less pressure will be needed here to instill a sense of safety and maintain a good level of comfort. Adjust the positioning of your own body as needed for your own comfort as well. Now take your three deep breaths, and on the exhalation, increase the pressure ever so slightly. If it feels good to do so, you can move your hand in a subtle circular shape on their chest. Remember, your intention is to soothe.

Finally, place your two hands on your partner's chest just under their collarbone. Repeat your sequence of breathing and pressure with gentle rocking motion to press or shake the tension out of their body.

We will complete this exercise by returning to your partner's head. Reposition yourself where you started, at their head. Place one hand across their forehead and apply gentle pressure. Pause here for a few moments. Then finish by running the fingers of both your hands through your partner's hair (or scalp).

Vulva Massage

Begin your experience by choosing a place and creating a special atmosphere. Dim the lights, burn incense or diffuse essential oils, light candles, play sexy or relaxing music. You might consider building a special "nest" on the floor with blankets and pillows. You can also set up on the bed. Either way, make sure you put a towel down to protect the surface from massage oil. You can use your favorite massage oil. I prefer coconut oil because it has a great consistency, spreads easily, and smells delicious. Keep a bowl of it next to you to dip into throughout the massage as needed to keep your hands moving smoothly across your partner's skin.

Context is important in creating a safe space for the vulnerability of a vulva massage. Create a place in which they can lie comfortably. Although it's fine to do this on a bed, it's nice to choose a spot on the floor to create a special nest, arranging blankets and pillows to support your partner comfortably. They should be lying on their back with a pillow to support each knee when their legs are spread and one under their head if they prefer to have it slightly raised.

Before you begin, take a few moments to connect with your partner by taking three deep, slow breaths together. Doing this will put you both at ease. Throughout the massage, keep reminding them to breathe, relax, and receive.

The most important thing to know is that all attention is on the person receiving the massage. There is nothing that you are doing for the purposes of your own physical pleasure or sexual satisfaction. Your entire focus is on delivering a gentle, positive, and healing experience for them. As you are about to get started, ask for permission to touch their body. Even though you have agreed to do this together, go through the formality of asking explicitly at the moment you are about to begin. Also, assure them that you will stop immediately if they indicate to do so at any point. When they are settled, situate yourself kneeling at their side.

Gently rub your hands together to warm them and place them on their shoulders. Gently massage the flesh on their shoulders, arms, hands, thighs, shins, ankles, and feet. Bring all your attention and intention to making them feel safe and held in this space. Let your hands be gentle enough to calm them and firm enough to reassure them.

As you feel your partner relax under your touch, leave one hand on them and dip the other in the bowl of coconut oil. Drizzle the oil on their abdomen around their navel. Gently spread the oil on their belly. Spend a few moments here, building the level of trust and ease.

When you feel them melt into the sensation, draw your hands down to their lower belly and hips. Let the arch of their back and the rise of their pelvis tell you when it's time to touch their inner thighs. Add coconut oil as needed to keep your hands slipping comfortably over their skin. As the heat in their body builds, your hands should be on their inner thighs, hips, lower belly, and pubic bone. You will want to reposition yourself so that you are kneeling between their legs. And now, if their legs are still needing to be opened, use one hand to gently guide their knees wider. Make sure they are comfortably propped up by the pillows you had placed close by. Do your best to always keep one hand on your partner so that they feel connected and held.

Now with one hand on each of their inner thighs, increase the pace of your strokes and allow the energy to build. There's no need to get anywhere. Be present in each moment as you create a slow, delicious build. Allow your partner's body to speak to you, to be your partner in stirring their arousal.

Gradually move your hands to the outer lips of their vulva. Place your well-oiled thumbs on either side of their vulva and move them up and down slowly. Listen for their cues and responses to the speed and pressure you use. Gently caress the folds of their inner and outer labia.

With your fingers well lubricated, place your nondominant hand just above their pubic bone and take the middle finger of your other hand and place it at the very top of their vulva above their clitoris. Slooowly press downward, gently parting their lips, and stroke the shaft of their clitoris and then circle it with your finger. Pay close attention to their level of pleasure and comfort. Some vulvas are more sensitive than others. Your partner should be experiencing extreme pleasure at this point. If they aren't, back off their clitoris and move to the folds of their labia. Make sure to keep the area well oiled to avoid too much friction.

Every vulva is unique. Be present to them, and tune into what they are feeling, the way they move and react to the various ways you are touching them. Ride a wave of sensation with them. Let your partner's body and vocalizations guide you as you cycle through stimulating all the various parts of their vulva.

When your partner is fully aroused, they might appear to be having an orgasm. You might not be able to tell for sure. That's okay. This kind of touch will often produce a full-body orgasm, a multiple orgasm, or a rolling orgasm. Just let your partner feel all the sensations of pleasure without having to define or name them. The goal is not to climax, but to feel an unparalleled amount of pleasurable sensation.

To complete this vulva massage, we are going to gradually stop stimulating the vagina. Slow it down. Take the heal of your hand and place it on your partner's pubic mound, placing gentle pressure against their outer labia with their clitoris underneath. Stay here for a full minute while their nervous system relaxes.

Return to the long firm massage strokes and gentle kneading of their thighs, arms, and hands. We are bringing your partner back into their body, letting them relax here as their breath lengthens and heart rate returns to normal. And if you are comfortable, you might end by gently stroking their hair or with a light kiss on their forehead.

Penis Massage

A penis massage isn't simply about having an orgasm, but about generating waves of orgasmic pleasure throughout the entire massage.

Begin your experience by choosing a place and creating a special atmosphere. Dim the lights, burn incense or diffuse essential oils, light candles, play sexy or relaxing music. You might consider building a special "nest" on the floor with blankets and pillows. You can also set up on the bed. Either way, make sure you put a towel down to protect the surface from massage oil. You can use your favorite massage oil. I prefer coconut oil because it has a great consistency, spreads easily, and smells delicious. Keep a bowl of it next to you to dip into throughout the massage as needed to keep your hands moving smoothly across the skin.

Have your partner lie on their back wherever and get comfortable. They might like a pillow under their head or under their hips, or both. Their legs should be spread apart with their knees bent, so you have easy access to all parts of their genitals. Before you begin, take a few moments to connect with your partner by taking three deep, slow breaths together. Doing this will put you both at ease. Throughout the massage, remind them to breathe, relax, and receive as needed.

You can perform a penis massage while kneeling or sitting by your partner's side, or you can kneel between their legs. Lubricate your hands, rubbing them together to warm them. Carefully avoid their genitals at first. Begin with long strokes to the tops of their thighs. Move these strokes toward their inner thighs, continuing to avoid touching their penis or testicles directly. Slide your hands up to their hip bones and finally their lower abdomen just above their pubic bone. Spend about two minutes lubricating and stroking these areas. Your partner may or may not have an erection at this point; either way is okay and normal.

When your partner is relaxed and accustomed to being touched, gently and slowly move on to their balls. You want to be careful here and really pay attention to the cues your partner is giving you. Individuals differ greatly as to the kind of touch they like. Some are more sensitive or ticklish than others. It's okay to check in with your partner as you begin.

With a well-lubricated hand, cup their testicles and gently massage them in the palm of your hand. With your fingertips flat against the skin of their scrotum, stroke the skin that connects their balls to their body. This skin is soft and tender. Move back and forth between cupping their balls and stroking the skin with flat fingertips. Rotate your hand so that your fingertips are on the underside of their scrotum and the heal of your hand is toward their penis. Very gently grab their ball sac and very slightly tug it away from their body. Some people love this, others not so much. Listen for your partner's cues. Do more of what they like and less of what they don't.

When you and your partner are comfortable with your handling their balls, massage the area behind their balls between the scrotum and anus. This is the perineum, or taint. It's a very sensitive area that can generate tremendous pleasure. The first touch should be with your flat fingertips. If your partner responds positively, you can gradually apply more pressure. This is the area where the prostate is located. The prostate gland can induce extreme states of pleasure if stimulated properly. For now, massage with your fingertips, pay attention, and let your partner's response guide you.

Next, move to the shaft of the penis. If they experience erection, your partner may be hard by now. Take your hand and place it palm up between their lower abdomen and their penis. With your other hand, place your entire palm on the underside of their penis, which is probably facing up. Spend a few moments simply holding their penis. Now slowly slide both hands in tandem up and down their penis. Vary the amount of pressure you are using.

Using your dominant hand, grab their shaft so that your fingers are against their belly, and rub your thumb up and down against the underside of their penis. Making sure you are well lubricated, zero in on the very sensitive area near the head. This is the glans of the penis, and it can generate a great deal of sensation. Work this area, paying attention to their response.

Now connect the tips of your thumb and fingers around the head of their penis and slide them up and down in a gentle tugging motion.

Bring your hand all the way off the end of their penis, and let the tip of their penis break through the grip of your hand, mimicking the opening of a vagina or anus. Add a rotation of the wrist to this motion.

Alternate this movement with long strokes up and down the length of their shaft. Add some gentle tugging on their balls with your other hand while you continue to rotate through various strokes on their penis.

Vary the speed from slow to fast. Start slowly and build up to a faster pace, then take it back to a slow speed again. Keep alternating the pressure, speed, rhythm, and strokes. Improvise, be creative, feel in the moment, tune into your partner, dance with the energy.

By now, they might be very worked up and want to come. If you are paying close attention to their breathing, how their body is moving, and their vocal cues, you should be able to predict if they're nearing orgasm. When you see them at that edge, back off a bit, or just slow it down. Remind them to breathe and ride the wave of orgasmic feelings they're experiencing. They might go from being rock hard to semihard and back again. That's totally normal.

To end the massage, you can either allow your partner to orgasm with ejaculation or move on to another form of pleasure.

WITH THE WORLD
Sensation Journal

We experience our world first and foremost through our five senses. If you spend time with an infant, this becomes immediately apparent. With limited cognition and the language to express it, the relationship between stimulus and reaction is instantaneous and simple. Physical intimacy with the world happens when you let it penetrate you through the vehicle of your five senses. I suggest keeping a special notebook or journal to track your impressions and hold yourself accountable. This exercise is best done daily for a period of one month.

- Make a note every day for each of your five senses of a moment in which you spent heightening your awareness of that sense.

- For instance, when you make your coffee in the morning . . .
  - Take a moment to experience fully the way the coffee beans smell. Notice the reaction of your body as the aroma penetrates your nostrils and makes its way to your brain.
  - Then as you take your first sip, notice the sound of your lips slurping to cool the hot liquid before it enters your mouth.
  - Notice the weight and warmth of the mug in your hand.
  - What color is your coffee? Is it rich brown like chocolate or potting soil? If you take your coffee with milk, how does it look when you pour the milk in and stir it?
  - Finally, of course, notice how it tastes as it bathes your taste buds with delicious flavor.
- Intimacy is available to you, even in your morning coffee ritual. Your sensation journal can repeat itself over and over, as long as the quality of your presence continues to grow over time.
- It can involve everyday mundane activities like brushing your teeth or making the bed, or you can take an epic adventure specifically for indulging the senses like a trip to a day spa or a hike through the forest.
- All five senses don't need to be logged from the same activity (like the coffee). In fact, it's even better if your awareness is spread out over many touchpoints throughout the day.

Walk Barefoot

The revolutionary Vietnamese Buddhist monk and activist Thich Nhat Hanh says, "We have to walk in a way that we only print peace and serenity on the Earth. Walk as if you are kissing the Earth with your feet."

Kiss Mother Earth and she'll return the favor. The formal practice is called *grounding*, and it's scientifically proven to be good for you. It's also referred to as *earthing* by enthusiasts. The idea is that in the industrial age, thanks to buildings, furniture, vehicles, and shoes with insulated synthetic soles, we have lost our direct and sustained connection to the subtle electric charge of Earth's surface. Walking barefoot has the beneficial physiological effect of acting as an antioxidant by neutralizing those dangerous free radicals that cause aging, cancer, chronic inflammation, and other diseases. Regular connection between the surface of our feet and the surface of Earth is shown to help regulate our circadian rhythm. This in turn regulates our autonomic nervous system, which governs our body temperature, blood pressure, hormone secretion, digestion, and sleep patterns.

Here's how you do it:

- Go outside and find a patch of grass, dirt, sand—even pavement will do if you're in the city. Take your shoes off and stand or walk.
- Aim to accumulate a total of thirty to sixty minutes of barefootedness each week.
- A period of at least thirty minutes is most powerful, so shoot for one of those each week.

If it's not possible for you to stand or walk, you can achieve the same benefits by sitting or lying down directly on grass, sand, or a blanket. If you cannot or do not want to make physical contact with the ground, simply being outdoors will suffice.

PART FOUR

ENERGETIC INTIMACY

CHAPTER 10

THE SPACE IN BETWEEN

EMILY AND MATTHEW ARE THE COUPLE YOU MET IN CHAPTER 6 WHO were dealing with a discrepancy in their level of desire for sex. While Matthew was working on owning his own feelings and becoming emotionally independent, Emily was looking at why she was so shut down to Matthew sexually. She rarely wanted sex, while her husband had the libido of a teenage boy, as she put it. She perceived that Matthew was ruled by his emotions and impulses. She observed this spilling over into his parenting. He often riled up their two young daughters when they should've been winding down for the night. He let them eat junk food and often behaved like a third child.

"I feel like the only adult in the home," Emily tells me. "I often feel like I am living in chaos. When I try to point it out, I sound like a nagging wife and mother," she says. "Inevitably, it leads to a big argument."

"What does that look like?"

"Well, usually it's Matthew feeling criticized and telling me I'm a control freak." I can hear the frustration in her voice. She goes on, "I mean, maybe I *am* controlling. I don't think so, but I am uncomfortable with how erratic and unpredictable he is and the effect it has on our home environment."

"Say more. What are some examples?" I prompt.

"Well, Matthew is a compulsive shopper. He will go to the Home Depot or Target and come home with all kinds of things. Not just for himself, but for the kids, the house . . . even me! Things we don't need; things I don't want. Our garage is jam-packed with *stuff.* He never asks me before he spends money. I am sure he has no idea how much he spends."

"Do you have a financial plan or a budget that you've created together, or agreed on?" I inquire.

"No . . . I have been bugging him to call an accountant who was recommended to us, but he hasn't followed through." Emily sounds deflated. "Matthew makes a lot of money. He has been really successful in his business as a commercial real-estate broker, so I think he just feels like we have enough money that we don't need to worry about how much we spend."

"How do you feel about it?" I already know the answer, but I want her to articulate it.

"Honestly, it makes me nervous not to have a financial plan that covers us for the future. You never know what will happen in the real-estate market. The money Matthew currently makes might change drastically at some point. And then where will we be? I think I am just not comfortable flying by the seat of our pants the way he is. Does that make me a control freak?" she asks earnestly.

"What I hear is someone who is strategic and responsible. I can see your desire to take advantage of Matthew's abundant income while it's there. That sounds smart and mature to me," I offer. "Emily, how do you think this contributes to your lack of desire for sex with Matthew?"

She pauses thoughtfully. "I think the best way to say it is that I don't feel safe."

"What do you mean by that exactly?" I ask.

"Matthew's energy in bed is the same thing. It feels like he is out of control. Like if I need him to stop or slow down, he won't be able to."

"Is this something you fear, or does this actually happen?"

"Well, it doesn't happen now because I just don't have sex with him if he is wound up. In the past there have been a few times when I have tried to communicate with him to slow down or ease up, but I feel like he just doesn't really see or hear me."

"Describe what you mean by 'wound up.'"

"Often, like a few times a week, he gets all horny. He talks about how much he wants me and how much my body turns him on. That sounds like it's a good thing, but he sounds like the cliché construction worker yelling to a woman walking by. I feel objectified, like he is turned on by my body and not by me. And there is an urgency to it, like his life depends on having sex with me. It feels like he's about to devour me. I have gotten to the point where it's just too exhausting to try to control his energy from the receiving end."

"What happens when you try to talk to Matthew about the way you feel?" I ask.

"He gets angry. He feels rejected and criticized. It's a consistent dynamic all the way around, in and out of the bedroom. Sometimes I think we are simply mismatched. I really love Matthew. He has many wonderful qualities. We are closely aligned in so many ways, but I think our styles are opposite. I'm not sure how we can come together."

"Tell me what you love about Matthew." I am curious.

"I love that he is passionate about his work. He's thoughtful and creative, and his partners and employees love him. I love the way he interacts with the girls. He is a playful and adventurous dad. That's something he brings to the family that I don't. I'm more serious." She goes on, "I love his political views. We share values and a kind of worldview. We have been through a lot together and have really grown up together in a lot of ways. I want this to work. I almost feel like I'd be okay if he got his sexual needs met elsewhere."

"And what about your needs, Emily?"

"My need is to be relieved of the pressure to have sex!" Her laugh doesn't mask the accuracy of her statement. She really is longing to be left alone in the bedroom. "It's just not that important to me."

Though there is truth in Emily's hypothesis that she and Matthew are stylistically mismatched, there is much to feel good about in their marriage. I am convinced there is a mutual love and respect for each other, and together they have created a cohesive and nurturing world for their daughters. I feel hopeful there is something we can do to bridge the divide.

"Emily, you mentioned energy. Can you give me three words you would use to describe Matthew's energy in the marriage apart from sex?" I inquire.

She is quick to answer: "Erratic, explosive, and unpredictable."

"And how would you like his energy to feel?"

"Solid, consistent, easeful. Hmmm . . . I like that." She smiles.

"And what are three words you would use to describe Matthew's energy in the bedroom?"

"Big, intense, overwhelming."

"And how would you like his energy to feel in the bedroom?"

"Controlled, smooth, and connected."

"You're doing a great job. Now tell me about your energy."

"In my marriage, I often feel contracted, irritated, and exhausted. I'd like to feel open, flowing, and expansive."

"And during sex?"

"I mostly feel guarded and shut down. I'm not sure how I would like to feel, maybe relaxed and playful. I haven't felt that way in a long time."

I took notes as Emily was talking, and we spent some time comparing how she felt and how she wanted to feel, and then we brought Matthew into the fold to share with us his perspective and needs. For Matthew and Emily, working on their dynamic through the lens of the energy they each brought to the equation opened a doorway to a conversation that had been previously fraught with emotion. What had been an argument about the level of entitlement Matthew displayed to his wife's body became an exploration of how to create a space in which she felt safe enough to invite him in. Matthew and Emily are a good example of what often happens with a long-term monogamous couple. Over time we begin to think we know everything there is to know about our partner. There are very few surprises. Especially when the care and raising of kids are a part of the equation, and time and space are at a premium, we lose the sense of autonomy that allows for mystery, intrigue, and discovery.

Esther Perel says in her seminal book, *Mating in Captivity: Reconciling the Erotic and the Domestic*, "Eroticism thrives in the space between the self and the other."

It is in this space, between two people, between thoughts and words, between the ideas of right and wrong, should and shouldn't, this or that, where there exists an opportunity to cultivate not only eroticism and desire but also a connection that exists outside of personality, role, history, and emotions. Adopting a perspective in which we meet each other like this, soul-to-soul, opens up the possibility to reinvent the way we relate to each other by reorganizing and redefining the assumptions, agreements, and structures on which the relationship is built. We can hardly demand that our partner want to have sex with us, but we can intentionally create the conditions in which their natural desire can flourish. In Matthew and Emily's case, this meant seeing each other with fresh eyes, recognizing their different styles as contributions rather than challenges, and creating opportunity to honor, respect, and capitalize on their individual strengths for the benefit of the relationship, which becomes a third entity alongside each of them as individuals.

Sometimes a *feeling* is neither emotional nor physical—a hunch, glimmer, notion, flash, intuitiveness, frisson, a feeling in your bones. I am guessing you can identify the existence of such phenomena in your life. Sometimes, this kind of feeling is based on a single or repeated experience that provides us the ability to anticipate the way a similar situation is about to unfold, like the predictive text function on a smartphone. But often, it feels like a kind of intuitive sense comes over us—or through us—from somewhere beyond our familiar cognitive faculties. Because this information arrives outside the realm of what we can see, hear, feel, smell, or touch, it's often referred to as a "sixth sense." While our primary five senses fall squarely in what we know to be the physical realm, the sixth can be categorized as *metaphysical*. Hang on, and bear with me. I am not about to take a left turn into the land of moonbeams and spirit guides. No one has ever accused me of being woo-woo, not even in the spiritual circles I have been known to frequent on the Westside of Los Angeles. If you want to understand how to feel more deeply connected in your experience of life, *energy* is the piece most commonly missing from the conversation. In my personal experience and professional expertise, it's equally essential as the psychology and physiology of intimacy.

Metaphysics is a term originating in the mid-sixteenth century referring to the Greek *ta meta ta phusika*, "the things after physics," later interpreted as meaning "the science of things transcending what is physical or natural." Though the term *metaphysical* is often used in conjunction with paranormal activity and psychic phenomena, it's actually a philosophical discipline rooted in science. Metaphysics is the branch of philosophy concerned with the nature of existence. It's the foundation on which all other discussions are built, which is why Aristotle calls it the "first philosophy" or sometimes simply "wisdom."

Energy is recognized in many parts of the world as a legitimate and intrinsic part of overall health and wellness of the human body and mind. In fact, energy is the central focus of most Eastern disciplines of medicine and physiology. In traditional Chinese medicine, everything is made up of qi, life-force energy. Balanced and abundant qi is the key to good health—mentally, physically, and emotionally. All physical ailments are a result of an imbalance in qi. Qi is balanced through acupuncture, herbs, tai chi, qigong, meditation, and diet. Similarly, the basis of wellness in traditional Indian medicine is the balance of energy. Ayurveda defines a complex system of three energy principles in the body: *vata*, *pitta*, and *kapha*, as well as universal life-force energy, *prana*. The yogic system of physiology names seven energy centers in the body, called chakras, which essentially run the length of the spine, starting at the genitals and sacrum and ending at the crown of the head. Vibrant health in all aspects depends on the ability of energy to flow freely up and down the chakras through channels on either side of the spine. The energetics of human physiology is considered such a significant part of existence, it is referred to as the *subtle body*. The solid, perishable body is called the *gross body*, while the subtle body lives on after death, merging back into the energy of the universe.

As Albert Einstein puts it, "Everything is energy and that's all there is to it. Match the frequency of the reality you want, and you cannot help but get that reality. It can be no other way. This is not philosophy."

You might be someone who feels deeply connected to their intuition and relies on it regularly as a navigational tool in orienteering your life. Most of us live in a world in which our thoughts, ideas, and decisions rely heavily on that which we know because we experience it directly with one or more of our five senses. We don't have a direct experience outside these parameters that we trust. It's only through the filter or translation of a priest, minister, rabbi, imam, or other religious leader that we are willing to trust that which cannot be proven. I am not invalidating such bringers of divine mystery into our lives. I am simply saying our full experience of radical intimacy is dependent on our willingness to embrace the reality of something we can directly feel ourselves, *even though* we cannot empirically verify, prove, or qualify its existence. There is a space between science and the divine, between intellectual and spiritual, between factual and woo-woo. It's in this in-between space that you'll find great opportunity for a dimensional shift of your relationship with yourself, others, and the world.

What does this look like in a rubber-hits-the-road kind of way? For one thing, it means that you can walk into a room and feel the energy. Think about how different it feels to walk into a yoga class versus a funeral versus a room full of high school seniors taking the SAT. Of course, you can observe what these three distinct groups of people are doing, the expressions on their faces, and the ways in which they are communicating with each other (or not). You can deduce and maybe even attune to their mental and emotional states, collectively and individually. However, additionally, there is an energy in the space that exists beyond the collection of people in the room. That energy might feel tense, congested, heavy, or it might feel open, expansive, buoyant. If you say that the room filled with mourners felt sad, you are talking about emotion, not energy. Energetically, that same room felt dense and heavy, which perhaps resulted in your feeling sad (emotionally) and disoriented (physically). The energy in the yoga studio was expansive and clear, which resulted in your feeling joyful and alive.

The same goes for your own personal energy. You might be grappling with a situation in which you feel stuck and unable to make a decision. The energy you feel is stagnant and stale. The emotions you feel are depressed and confused, whereas physically you feel anxious and tired. We can look for the energy of an experience alongside the physical and the emotional. While our physical world is completely objective, our emotional world is fully subjective. Our energetic world lies somewhere in between. The distinction between emotions and energy in the way we feel offers two different ways to evaluate both the content and the context of a current circumstance. The additional perspective energy provides can be tremendously helpful, especially when emotions are running high. I often work with clients to understand their circumstances through the lens of the energy they feel as opposed to the energy they *want* to feel.

Matthew learned to anchor his expansive energy with the disciplined structure of regular workouts at the gym, an organized way of managing shopping, and finally enlisting the support of a financial adviser to create both a household budget and sustainable wealth. Emily learned to free up her controlled energy by having daily spontaneous ten-minute dance parties with the kids as well as attending weekly ecstatic dance sessions herself. She also experimented with going grocery shopping without a list. When it came to sex, we developed specific guidelines for behavior and verbal expression for each of them that cultivated energy conducive to connection rather than conflict. For instance, rather than ogling Emily's body, Matthew took time each night to tell Emily at least one thing he admired or appreciated about her (apart from the way she looked). For her part, Emily initiated some kind of nonsexual physical contact with Matthew each day, like a hug or a massage, which made him feel cared for and satisfied his need to feel soothing energy. I had them schedule sex to interrupt their pattern of request and rejection and reduce the risk of emotional upset. Each of them was responsible for initiating on one of those two days. When it was Matthew's turn, he was to slow way down and ask for consent before acting. There were specific things Emily knew would help her relax and connect. She shared them with her husband, and they agreed to frame their lovemaking as a collaborative exercise in shaping the energy so they each felt safe and inspired. When it was Emily's turn to initiate, she got to choose whether to give or receive and what activities they would indulge in. Intercourse was not required, and it was up to her to decide if she wanted to feel any degree of sexual pleasure herself or simply pleasure Matthew. This worked to equalize the power in their sexual dynamic, which became a launchpad for the rest of their marriage.

A different way energy can manifest in the realm of sexuality is found in Harriet's story. Harriet is an accomplished forty-two-year-old woman who has run a corporation since she was twenty-four years old. Her awards and accolades speak to her brilliance. Everyone from her board of directors to the PTO president at her daughter's school knows that if you want to get something done, call Harriet. She came to me because she was struggling to make sense of something she was experiencing sexually.

"Where would you like to begin, Harriet?" I ask in our first session.

"I am struggling with my desire to be dominated in bed. It doesn't fit with who I think I am," she explains. "I am a dyed-in-the-wool feminist. I am one of the most competent women I know. I am a living testament to the fact that a woman does not need a man. I even had a child on my own with the help of a sperm bank."

"Harriet, what is your orientation? Are you a lesbian?" I ask.

"No, I'm not. I like men just fine, but it's rare to find one who can accept my independence. There isn't much room in my life for a partner. Most of the men I've dated have trouble with that. And to be honest, I am fine with having lovers who don't necessarily become full-on relationships. I wouldn't get married anyway. I don't believe in it as an institution."

"Fair enough. So, what are you making your desire to be dominated mean about you?"

"Well, to be honest, I am embarrassed. For years I have fantasized about what might even be characterized as rape. Now, for the last three months, I've been dating a man who ties me up and flogs me, and I'm a little horrified to admit that I love it. I never thought of myself as kinky. I am confused about why it would turn me on to be dominated by a man when I am the living embodiment of female power."

"I can see that you're angry," I observe.

She takes a deep breath and sighs. "I am angry. I'm not sure why."

"Very often, anger arises when one or more of our values are being violated. In this case, your sexual desire is bumping up against your value of gender equality."

"Yes! That's right, and it's coming from the inside. I have no one to be mad at but myself."

"Harriet, are you familiar with the adage: *How you do anything is how you do everything?*" I ask.

"Yes, I say it all the time," she responds.

"I like to add the words *except in bed* to the end. How you do anything is how you do everything, except in bed. It's often true that the very thing we find erotic is the opposite of what we want in our real lives."

"Huh . . ." I can almost hear her synapses firing.

"Our experience of sex is so much richer when we give ourselves permission to explore our sexual identity as something that exists separate from our professional or family identities. Think about it. How you show up as a CEO is different from how you show up as a mother, yes?"

"Yes, pretty much, but though my manner and behavior change, they are both informed by a value system that stays intact." She makes a good point.

"What if being dominated in bed doesn't actually violate that value system?"

"I don't follow."

I proceeded to have Harriet describe her day to me. Between work and single motherhood, she was not only busy, but carried an enormous amount of responsibility for the well-being of a great many people. She took that responsibility seriously, and it informed her actions all day long as she went from one meeting to another, making big decisions that would affect the lives of her employees and their families. She spent a lot of time in her head, figuring things out, strategizing, collaborating, and communicating. I asked her how she felt at the end of a typical day, and her answer was telling.

"Like my head is going to explode," she says. "By the time I get home to my daughter, I am exhausted, and I can't stop thinking all at the same time."

"I can imagine," I respond. "Harriet, how do you feel after you have sex with your new lover?"

"Exactly the opposite. Like I don't have a thought in my head. It's almost like I don't have a head at all. I'm alive and energized and completely in my body."

"Beautiful! It makes sense that you would need to discharge that energy from time to time. In effect, you are resetting your nervous system," I suggest.

"It does make perfect sense, actually," she agrees.

"So, what if you own your kink as an intentional way of managing your energy? Being dominated is your choice. Not only are you consenting, but you're cocreating an arrangement in which you relinquish control. Your submission is a release, and your partner is holding a container in which you are safe to let go."

"You're blowing my mind. It makes so much sense," Harriet says.

"One of the things that is widely misunderstood about BDSM is that it's the submissive who really holds the power. On the surface it looks like the Dominant who holds the power, but actually the Dom/sub relationship is highly nuanced and consensual. The Dom's power is asserted at the request of and in service of the sub."

"I feel much better about all this. Thank you for reframing it. This is actually really exciting."

Understanding her kink as a practice that nourishes her nervous system helped Harriet let go of her shame and embrace her self-expression fully and safely.

Emily's and Harriet's stories are just two examples of a myriad of ways energy plays a part in our intimate relationships, sexual and otherwise. I invite you to consider situations in your life in which energy might play a significant part of your experience. How does the distinction between energy and emotion affect the way you see, understand, and interpret what is actually happening? What is the difference between the way you feel energetically and emotionally about a situation or inside a relationship? Does anything get freed up by shifting your focus from an emotional experience to an energetic one?

CHAPTER 11

THE ATTACHMENT MYTH

THE CONFLATION OF ENERGY AND EMOTION HAS LED TO ONE OF the biggest limiting beliefs in our culture. There is a pervasive conviction that women become emotionally attached to their sexual partners and categorically require emotional intimacy in order to enjoy sex. Specific to the cisgender, heterosexual population, this untruth, which I call "the Attachment Myth," seems to be perpetuated and reinforced at every turn. Those who subscribe to theories of evolutionary psychology will tell you that in order for the species to survive, males are driven to plant their seed in as many women as possible. For females, it is advantageous that the male stick around and continue to provide for the family. In order to feel paternal ownership, it is imperative that the male partner be sure he is the father. This argument has been used forever not only to explain but to justify why men have a penchant for having sex outside their long-term monogamous relationships, often with partners with whom they aren't emotionally involved. Women, on the other hand, have no such evolutionary reasons for having sex outside the marriage, so they are stuck at home waiting for their ride-or-die to come back after spreading his seed elsewhere. Christopher Ryan and Cacilda Jethá blow up this simplistic theory in their book, *Sex at Dawn: How We Mate, Why We Stray, and What It Means for Modern Relationships*, which I highly recommend if you want to dive deeper.

Religious institutions with patriarchal underpinnings have good reason to perpetuate the Attachment Myth. Already concerned with the distraction of sexual desire in its male leaders and their constituents, it's important to suppress the sexual expression of its women. It's much easier to control men's desire if the women in the community are not readily available because they require a good deal of work in the form of emotional activation prior to sex. The foundation of biblical culture, after all, is the blame of Eve for the temptation of Adam, but it's not just Western religion that brainwashes women into believing their sexual freedom is dependent on their emotional enslavement. I sat in a workshop at a yoga festival several years ago given by a well-known and respected yoga teacher who is a direct disciple of renowned scholar and master of Indian philosophy Tirumalai Krishnamacharya. I was a fan of this yoga teacher I'll refer to as Walt. He taught a very simple form of yoga that, in many ways, gave me my practice back after navigating for years what had become an industry of fashion and influencers. Walt was known to speak about love and sex, and I was interested to hear his yogic perspective of such human endeavors. It turned out Walt did very little teaching. The workshop took the form of a group discussion in which I heard significantly more thoughts and musings of the attendees than I did wisdom and teachings from Walt. Just about none of it stays with me now years later except one outrageous statement that makes me angry to this day. While I can't remember the context, the following words came out of Walt's mouth and etched themselves on my psyche as a permanent call to action to dismantle the patriarchy.

"Every time a woman has intercourse with a man, his energy stays in her body for seven years. A woman takes on the karma of every man with whom she has sex," Walt said.

"What kind of fucked up bullshit is that?!" I thought to myself and then subsequently expressed to the group. "What *man* made that crap up to keep women from embracing their sexuality for pleasure and empowerment?" Later that day, another teacher happened to reveal that he won't sleep in bed with his wife when she menstruates because a woman's vibration is too low when she bleeds. The high-vibe miracle of the female body is the fact that the womb is the site of the very moment the sacred meets the profane in the form of new life . . . but that's a different book.

You don't have to go to a church or a yoga festival to find the substrata of the Attachment Myth. It's coming through your streaming devices constantly in the content you consume. Whether it's a diet of rom-coms or reality TV you are snacking on, there is a pervasive message that women who require emotional connection for physical intimacy are more honorable than women who do not. The same is not true of men in the "boys will be boys" and "bros before hoes" subtext of popular culture. Osmosis provides a powerful and steady infusion of the idea that for men, sex is a purely physical phenomenon and for women it is inherently emotional. This is a gross generalization that depends on way more than the survival of our Neanderthal ancestors, the anatomy and physiology of our brains, or religious stories that support the dominance and superiority of men. While there is definitely truth in the idea that women thrive on love and connection, there is tremendous latitude in how that might inform our social structures and systems.

Cultures all over the world are structured around women having uncommitted multiple sex partners without sustained monogamous emotional attachment. You might be familiar with the Mosuo, a tribe who live in southwest China at the foot of the Tibetan Himalayas. They are mostly located in the provinces of Yunnan and Sichuan, on the shores of the paradisiacal Lugu Lake. The Mosuo, who refer to themselves as the Na, describe their culture as one of love, equality, and nonviolence. Known as the "Kingdom of Women," women are free to have multiple partners and to initiate or terminate relationships as they please. Men pay secret nocturnal visits to the women, who choose whether to let them in. They practice what is called "walking marriage," which doesn't include cohabitation and looks very much like the relationship we know of as that of a boyfriend/girlfriend. A woman can stay in her walking marriages as long or short as she likes. It's quite normal for a woman to have multiple relationships with men simultaneously and sequentially. Walking marriages are based on mutual affection and can last a day or a lifetime.

What facilitates this practice is a socioeconomic structure that supports the empowerment of women. Children belong to their mothers and are raised communally by their maternal extended family. Women own land, run businesses, and participate in government. Although the fathers of children are identified, they do not participate directly in their raising and care. Rather, they help to raise their nieces and nephews. All this is to say, the Na women are not dependent on the financial support of the fathers of their children, freeing them to make choices independent of economic criteria. The Mosuo women live in a culture that gives them permission to express themselves sexually in a context that isn't burdened by the fulfillment of sustained emotional need.

Let me be clear. I'm not making the argument that women should start having sex indiscriminately. I'm suggesting that on the individual and cultural levels, we have a gross misunderstanding of the nature of love and connection.

Widely known physician and psychiatrist David R. Hawkins was a pioneer in the intersection of medicine, psychology, and human consciousness. In 1973, he coauthored the groundbreaking work *Orthomolecular Psychiatry* with Nobel Laureate chemist Linus Pauling, initiating a new field within psychiatry. His perspective on love is that it's not an emotion. Although it can stir an emotional response, love itself is the embodiment of an idea, a perspective. He says, "Love is misunderstood to be an emotion; actually, it is a state of awareness, a way of being in the world, a way of seeing oneself and others."

Hawkins's view of love is echoed by many, from experts in the fields of science, spirituality, philosophy, psychology, and self-development. In his book *Be Love Now: The Path of the Heart*, author and teacher Ram Dass elaborates on the idea that love isn't an emotion: "Love is actually part of you; it is always flowing through you. It's like the subatomic texture of the universe, the dark matter that connects everything. When you tune into that flow, you will feel it in your own heart—not your physical heart or your emotional heart, but in your spiritual heart, the place you point to in your chest when you say, 'I am.'" He goes on to say, "Unconditional love really exists in each of us. It's part of our deep inner being. It's not so much an active emotion as a state of being."

The common narrative about feeling, giving, and receiving love to an object of our affection diminishes what's possible relationally, but also creates a schism in our understanding of ourselves in the context of the world. When we limit the experience of love to be transactional, we deny ourselves access to the infinite well of love available to us in every moment, whether we engage with another person or not. In other words, being in a constant state of unconditional love means we show up to our relationships, sexual and otherwise, whole and complete, free and at choice. The moral burden and shame of sex without love that keep us from uninhibited sexual expression are eradicated by the simple fact that there is always love. When we recognize that love is not dependent on a giver and receiver but rather the willingness to exist as the energy of love, then sex without love ceases to exist.

Now let's take a look at the nature of connection. If I had a dime for every time a woman said to me that she needs to feel "emotionally connected" to her lover in order to enjoy sex, I'd be able to feed a small nation.

University of Houston research professor and thought leader Brené Brown has spent decades studying courage, vulnerability, shame, and empathy. She defines *connection* as "the energy that exists between people when they feel seen, heard, and valued; when they can give and receive without judgement; and when they derive sustenance and strength from the relationship."

What Brown is describing here is presence, something Buddhist meditation teacher Tara Brach defines as "the felt sense of wakefulness, openness, and tenderness when we are fully here and now." That earth-shattering, soul-shaking, mind-blowing feeling of great sex doesn't require the engagement of emotion. In fact, it's the result of an energetic connection that transcends emotion.

Now, for a number of reasons, you may specify the presence of emotional intimacy as a prerequisite for sex. That's a perfectly legitimate choice. But let that decision come from informed intention, not from the internalized idea that powerful, healthy sexual expression is dependent on emotional entanglement. In fact, it's just the opposite. Sex is most powerful when we are able to step beyond thought and emotion and be fully present. It's easy to see how this misinterpretation causes suffering as it plays out in Maddie's story, which is archetypal in its portrayal of the Attachment Myth.

Maddie was an acquaintance who reached out to me to talk through a pattern that had developed in her life. At the time that we spoke, she was confused, discouraged, and disappointed in men. In the prior two years, she had had a series of six relationships, all of which ended abruptly and painfully for her. Her repeated experience was that the spark, which had initially been strong, fizzled quickly before it had a chance to grow into a sustainable fire. In each of her six recent experiences, it was the men who either walked away or reneged on the terms of their agreement. She was building a case based on this evidence that all men are emotionally unavailable and resistant to commitment.

"I've been riding an emotional roller coaster in these last few years, and I don't know why the same thing keeps happening," Maddie explains.

"Can you describe what it is that keeps happening?" I inquire.

"I meet a guy; we hit is off; there's incredible chemistry; I think to myself, 'This could be the one,' and then we have sex, and it's all downhill from there."

"Like right away?" I ask.

"It's usually within days or weeks that we start arguing, and it reaches a point of no return. Either they break it off, or they say things that are so hurtful that I can't stay," she shares. "It feels like I am either euphoric or devastated. I can't do this anymore. Is it me? Is it them?"

"Tell me about sex. Is that happening quickly?" I ask.

She laughs. "Well, I love sex, so I tend to have sex quickly. Sometimes right away; sometimes I try to wait a few dates. Good chemistry can be irresistible!"

"It's wonderful that you are so connected to your sexuality and can easily express yourself in that way," I offer.

"The thing is, I fall in love as soon as I have sex. I can't help it. I am just wired that way."

We went on to talk about her "wiring" and who she thought installed it. After exploring some of her sexual influences, Maddie says to me, "I guess if I waited longer to have sex, I could see if a guy had staying power."

"Meaning, if you mean, 'Why buy the cow if the milk's free?' Let's pull this apart a little before you start basing choices on old clichés. Tell me about falling in love when you have sex. What is it you are actually falling in love with?"

"Well, I think I am falling in love with them. What do you mean?" She's not defensive, but genuinely puzzled.

"How much do you know about your partners at the time that you feel you are falling in love with them?"

"Huh. Not much, I guess," she realizes.

"Describe the feeling of love."

"Oh, wow. It's hard to put into words. I think it's that feeling of being really seen. There's a vulnerability and intimacy that makes my heart burst open."

"And when your heart bursts open, that's what you are calling 'falling in love'?" I clarify.

"Yes, I think so. It's hard to put words to feelings in this way. I never really thought that much about it. I just know that when I have that feeling, I want it to last forever," she shares.

"And it's your experience that your partners feel the same way?"

"Well, yeah. I mean, I can feel the connection. I am not sure about the 'last forever' part. It's been my experience that they lose interest." She goes on, "Maybe women are more emotionally needy than men. When I am in love with someone, I get attached to them. Isn't that how it works?"

"Are you attached to them, or are you attached to the idea that the feeling of love should last forever?" I challenge her, "Are you attached to the outcome of the story you're telling yourself about what it means to share a moment of connectedness?"

"Ouch," Maddie says.

"What hurts?" I ask.

"I think I have been making some assumptions not only about how my partners have felt but about how I feel too."

She's got it. "Tell me more," I encourage her.

"I make sexual chemistry mean everlasting love and assume my partner feels the same way. Then I get attached to my commitment to make it happen."

"Yes! So how do you shift your approach to relationship in order to find mutual love and commitment?"

"One way would be to wait to have sex until I find someone I get to know long enough to really love. I feel like it could take years to really find that person. Does that mean I don't have sex for years? I don't like that part."

"Or you could switch up the way you frame the connection you feel when you have sex."

"Tell me more," she says curiously.

"What if the love you feel doesn't have requirements attached to it? What if you recognize love as energy instead of emotion? What if what you are mistaking as emotional intimacy is actually energetic intimacy? Does that free you up to have sex without attachment to a story line that doesn't necessarily ring true?" I ask.

Maddie digests that for a while. It's a lot to take in.

Finally, she says, "I love this. This is huge. But I have to be honest and admit that I am still afraid I won't be able to handle my emotions."

"That's totally understandable, Maddie. The emotions that are stirred by powerful energetic intimacy are real. It's not that they go away. By parsing out the nature of energetic intimacy as something separate from emotional intimacy, you allow for two different experiences. You also recognize that the emotions you feel may or may not be shared by your partner. You have the opportunity to act accordingly, whatever the case."

"So how do I interrupt the old cycle, practically speaking?" she asks. "What actions do I take to do this differently?"

"That's a great question," I respond. "First of all, look to other places in your life that you can draw the distinction between energy and emotion. For instance, we live in Los Angeles. Every night for a week, go down to the beach and watch the sunset. Observe the beauty and magnificence of Mother Nature's display. See if in the experience of awe, you can identify both the feeling of energy and the subsequent feeling of emotion."

"This is good homework. I love the sunset," Maddie says.

"Great. So, consider witnessing the sunset as energetic intimacy with nature, or the universe. Be present to the sky in a way that brings a felt sense of wakefulness, an openness, a tenderness," I instruct. "Then, notice how and when that presence moves you emotionally. You might feel joy, bliss, overwhelmed, fear. Those are emotions."

"I get it. My emotions aren't *caused* by the sunset. They are a *result* of my energetic intimacy with the universe."

"It's a subtle distinction, but when you apply it to what's happening in your sex life, it becomes a powerful tool for managing your expectations and attachments," I respond. "You might decide that sex without true emotional intimacy and a relational contract brings with it more emotion than you care to manage in the aftermath. On the other hand, giving yourself permission to enjoy the combination of energetic and physical intimacy creates a certain responsibility and freedom that open up a whole new way of being."

Maddie went on to have a series of sessions with me to help her step into this new relational paradigm. Over the subsequent months, she became masterful at managing her own desire, energy, emotions, and expectations. There were times she slowed things down, taking time to draw distinctions and discernments, and there were times when she allowed a powerful experience to exist without the burden of making it conform to a happily-ever-after outcome. As this book goes to press, Maddie is in year two of a thriving committed partnership with a man who loves her deeply and is committed to enduring partnership.

The biggest tragedy of the Attachment Myth is that it has created throngs of women who have been systematically oppressed by the mischaracterization of their sexuality. In a cultural context, the indoctrination of women to believe they can—or *should*—express themselves sexually only under the preexisting conditions of relational commitment is a manifestation of the threat sexually empowered women pose to the patriarchy. The patriarchy by definition is a system in which men hold the majority of power, and women are excluded from it.

Rebecca Solnit, who originated the term *mansplain*, says in her book *Men Explain Things to Me*, "Every woman knows what I'm talking about. It's the presumption that makes it hard, at times, for any woman in any field; that keeps women from speaking up and from being heard when they dare; that crushes young women into silence by indicating, the way harassment on the street does, that this is not their world. It trains us in self-doubt and self-limitation just as it exercises men's unsupported overconfidence."

Though Solnit speaks to verbal expression here, the same is true for sexual expression. The most powerful way to accomplish the suppression of women's sexual sovereignty is by influencing their self-perception and, thereby, limiting their behavior. Drill this down and you end up with two groups of people, separated by culturally imposed gender identity, who relate to themselves and each other in accordance with two different sets of rules. The most important argument for the personal distinction of energy and emotion as it applies to sexuality is the liberation of individuals—regardless of gender—in the perception of themselves and the discovery of deeply nourishing expression and connection.

CHAPTER 12

A DEEP AND ABIDING PRESENCE

IN MODERN HISTORY, WE HUMANS HAVE BECOME HIGHLY INVESTED in the idea of connectivity. Our pursuit of it has focused mostly on technology in developing an expanding array of ways in which we can communicate with each other. In the stone age of modern technology, it was 1993 when the Internet first became available in a very limited form to the general public through the miracle of a dial-up modem (remember that dissonant tonal sound?!). By 2005 there were more than a billion Internet users worldwide. We've created broadband as a way to connect with a variety of devices simultaneously in multiple modalities. With the invention of tablets, watches, laptops, desktops, smartphones, TVs, and DVRs, we are well equipped with everything we need to connect with each other through words and pictures 24/7 at warp speed. All this connectivity has provided us efficiency, immediacy, and convenience. However, by and large, we haven't used the by-product of these gifts—additional time and space—to our advantage. We seem simply to fill it up with more activity.

There's an argument to be made that technology provides not only a way to get more done, but also the space to get more "undone." What I mean by this is that in the time we save using technology to manage our personal and professional lives, we could step away from all the "doing" and turn our attention to simply "being."

If you think about it, we spend a good portion of our lives reviewing, reevaluating, and reliving the past. The rest is spent envisioning, planning, and worrying about the future. It's not dishonorable that we want to learn from the past to create a bright future or that we have a cohesive vision for where we are going with a remembrance of where we've been. That kind of meta-view gives us valuable perspective. What we are seemingly (and woefully) inept at is the ability to be fully present in the moment. Most of us spread ourselves thin in the cultural phenomenon of multitasking, fracturing our attention and missing the fullness of each activity as it unfolds. In the quieter, simpler moments of our days, we tend to remain just as busy mentally, contextualizing each situation or conversation as a reflection of the past or prediction of the future. For most of us, there is a persistent internal negotiation of how to manipulate what's happening in any given moment to bring our desired outcome. We've been taught to decide what we want and how to make it happen and to be relentless in our focused pursuit of that goal. Ambition and drive are wonderful qualities to embody. The problem comes when, failing to recognize the limitations of our own knowledge and perspective, we operate without pausing to include the observation of evidence, contribution of cohorts, and the kind of deep listening that can happen only in stillness—all of which have the potential to steer our journey toward a more desirable destination, one we never even knew to imagine.

The three pillars of Energetic Intimacy are Presence, Humility, and Curiosity. Presence is the ability to step out of subjective interpretation and into objective observation. It's the state of total, nonjudgmental awareness moment to moment. Humility is the willingness to suspend the idea that we need to do or know anything. It's the state of surrender to being part of something bigger than ourselves. Curiosity is the eagerness to learn something new. It's the state of openness and interest.

If you are hiking in the woods and you see a tree on the trail up ahead, you might thoughtfully determine it's a sugar maple. It stands about twenty feet tall, and its leaves are just beginning to turn that brilliant shade of reddish orange, which means autumn is approaching. If you deepen your presence to the tree, in between the thoughts that convey your knowledge and experience, you will notice that it is a large mass mostly made of a hard substance, the surface of which is covered in a brown and gray thick, flaky texture. The flat mostly green pieces that appear to be growing from the extremities of the structure blow in the wind, which creates a gentle sound. If you close your eyes, you begin to hear this sound not as leaves rustling but as an abstract soundscape of aural sensation. The same is true for the smell and feel of this grand object as you experience it directly without the filter of your mind's interpretation.

To the extent that we are willing to disengage from our intellect (presence), step into the state of not-knowing (humility), and open fully to the sensorial experience (curiosity), we increase our capacity for intimacy.

The power of presence, humility, and curiosity is reflected in the Zen koan *The Tiger and the Strawberry*:

> A man was walking through a forest when he saw a tiger peering out at him from the underbrush. As the man turned to run, he heard the tiger spring to chase him. Barely ahead of the tiger, running for his life, the man came to the edge of a steep cliff. Clinging to a strong vine, he climbed over the edge of the cliff just as the tiger was about to pounce. There he was, dangling over the side of the cliff. He looked up and saw the hungry tiger pacing above him. He looked down and was dismayed to see *what would, undoubtedly, be a fatal fall.*
>
> Just then, a tiny mouse darted out from a crack in the cliff face above him and began to gnaw at the vine. At that precise moment, the man

noticed a wild strawberry sprouting from the vine. It was plump and perfectly ripe. He plucked it and popped it in his mouth.

It was incredibly delicious, the best strawberry he had ever had.

In this story, the man ate the strawberry in spite of his impending peril. That he dies relishing what he knows will be his last moments is a testament to the power of presence, humility, and curiosity. He might just as easily have squandered the opportunity for joy by fretting about how he got himself into this mess or worrying about what will happen next. On some level, he surrenders to the circumstance, of which he is just one part. Curiosity makes him open to experiencing the strawberry. It's through presence, humility, and curiosity that he's able to literally suck the juice out of every (last) moment.

I will never forget the watershed moment that personally brought home the power of presence and eventually led me to draw the distinction of energetic intimacy. It was in the months after a breakup with a man who was "just not that into me." I was devastated and trying to understand what I knew was a disproportionate degree of heartbreak for the circumstances. I happened upon an advertisement for a four-week tantra immersion with the controversial teacher Psalm Isadora. I signed up immediately with the intention of exploring the nature of intimacy and ways to balance what I thought of as the wholeness of self with the merging of another. In other words, *Why was it so easy to lose myself in someone else?* What I had no way of knowing was that this monthlong program would open the door to a world previously unknown to me and radically transform my own experience of myself in every sense. I ended up studying with Psalm for several years and was eventually initiated into the Sri Vidya lineage of tantra, which continues to inform much of my work today.

In this initial immersion, we met three times a week for four consecutive weeks. Thirteen of us spent a total of twenty-four hours together in the studio built out over the detached garage of the house in which Psalm lived, in Venice, California. Bathed in candlelight, we would start with meditation and breath work, followed by discussion. We rounded out each evening with a practice called Yab Yum. We paired off and sat face-to-face on the floor with legs wrapped around each other. Gazing into our partner's eyes, we breathed together and allowed creative life-force energy (essentially sexual energy) to build and circulate between us while Psalm chanted and sang mantras in the ancient language of Sanskrit. We switched partners twice, for a total of three twenty-minute "sits." The pairing-up process was random, self-managed, and messy. It was always a little nerve-racking to determine who would end up with whom. We each secretly had our favorite people to sit with. Some combinations felt more or less awkward than others. It was all part of the learning—comfort and discomfort were equally valuable experiences.

In the first three weeks, I managed to successfully avoid partnering with one of the participants I found utterly repugnant. There wasn't anything about Thomas I found redeeming. He was a self-centered, unattractive know-it-all. That last week, in the penultimate gathering, as we paired up in our usual disorganized fashion for our final partner exercise, the moment I dreaded became a reality: Thomas was my partner. Although by then I knew to recognize this as an opportunity, there was no way to know the impact of what was about to unfold. Like every other Yab Yum in the past several weeks, we sat facing each other, me on Thomas's lap with our legs wrapped around one another. Everything inside my chest and belly contracted like the face of a small child being forced to swallow a spoonful of medicine that tasted putrid. To say I was resistant is an understatement. I tried my best to simply focus on the physical sensation of my breath and to allow the breath to unclench the soft, tender center of body. As we sat there gazing into each other's eyes, little by little, with every breath, my ideas about Thomas dissolved; his costume of identity fell away. I saw the tenderness of his being, vulnerable and pure. It felt as if we were gazing into each other's souls. We were meeting in that field Rumi talks about, *out beyond ideas of wrongdoing and rightdoing*, and it was life changing.

I fell in love with Thomas that night. I mean, I was overcome with love, and it was undeniably mutual. The life-force energy we cultivated together in that twenty minutes was so abundant and strong we could easily have ripped each other's clothes off and made love right there on the studio floor. As the exercise came to a close, I was stunned. I couldn't believe this was the same man I detested. Nothing about what had just happened made sense. It had been easy enough to share this kind of experience with someone I liked and was predisposed to feel love and appreciation for, but to fall so deeply in love with someone whom I actively loathed was astonishing. This experience caused a monumental paradigm shift in the way I thought about human nature, love, energy, and intimacy. I had to ask myself: *If it was possible to love this invidious man, what else was possible?*

Thomas and I never knew each other more than we did that night. Our experience didn't translate to life outside the studio. He and I came from two different worlds. It would have defeated the whole point to attach some sort of story line or outcome to our experience, nor was I even tempted to. A couple of years later, we ran into each other on the street. He looked the same as he ever did, but when I laid eyes on him, I silently chuckled to myself how his affect had once offended me so. In that present moment, my heart swelled with love. To this day, I remain deeply grateful for his willingness to meet that night in a place where nothing existed except the wonder of another soul.

After my experience in Psalm's tantra immersion, I began to understand what Ram Dass meant when he said, "Treat everyone you meet like God in drag." I started assuming that anyone acting poorly is a worthy soul who is suffering in some way and lacks the skill to deal with it effectively. That guy driving next to me who gave me the finger was letting his own pain spill over onto me in the form of aggressive gestures. It really had nothing to do with me. I don't condone road rage, or aggression in general, but my new appreciation for people's souls—beyond the roles they play—opened a new way of being in the world. To this day, whenever someone flips me off, without one ounce of irony, I blow them a kiss and mouth the words, "I love you." This is significant for a woman who learned how to drive in New York!

There are certainly times when we are called upon to support someone in distress. Whether we walk the Buddhist path dedicated to relieving the suffering of all sentient beings or not, in these moments, presence, humility, and curiosity are a powerful combination. Often in this role, we misunderstand what is needed. In trying to be helpful, we jump into problem-solving mode, doing and saying whatever we think will make the target of our help feel better. To stop the pain, we amplify, blame, strategize, suppress. When performed unskillfully, our efforts to help or fix can cause more harm than good. In supporting someone in distress, we must be able to tolerate their discomfort in the name of their growth and evolution. Providing a safe, judgment-free environment or container is commonly referred to as "holding space." Though holding space requires a certain level of physical and emotional presence, it is primarily a form of energetic intimacy. Holding space means placing your attention on someone to support them as they feel, express, and process their thoughts and feelings. We can hold space for just about anyone—friends, lovers, family, colleagues, even strangers in need of support.

There are five key components to holding space skillfully:

1. **Shut Up and Listen:** Refrain from talking. When you do, use a minimum of words. Listen deeply. Don't spend your listening time thinking about what you're going to say next.
2. **Stay Steady:** Don't turn away, stay neutral, pay attention, and don't take on the emotions you are witnessing. Don't amplify; have boundaries.
3. **Don't Judge:** Don't judge the person you are supporting: their actions, thoughts, emotions, the situation, the other players in the story. Don't blame. Don't shame. Hold the highest good for all involved.
4. **Don't Center Yourself:** This is not the time to share your own similar experiences. Nor is it the time to talk about how hard it is to see your person in pain. Do not distract your person from their process by requiring them to take care of you.

5. **Don't Fix:** This is not a time to offer solutions, to strategize, to weigh in, to deny the facts, to analyze, to problem-solve. This includes avoiding platitudes like: *God only gives us what we can handle. What doesn't kill you makes you stronger. Everything happens for a reason.*

Built on a foundation of presence, humility, and curiosity, these five key components allow us to provide a deep and abiding presence that serves not only those for whom we hold space, but also ourselves as witnesses to life unfolding before our eyes. Whether it's a driver giving you the finger, a lover in the throes of passion, a friend who has suffered a loss, or the barista having a bad day, watch what happens when you bring your deep and abiding presence to the moment.

EXERCISES FOR CULTIVATING ENERGETIC INTIMACY

WITH SELF

Breath Work (Zazen Style)

We often use the term *Zen* to describe that state of unshakable inner peace and composure. Zazen is the meditation practice at the heart of Zen, a school of Buddhism that focuses on the study of the self. This simple practice will bring structure to the experience of solitude and stillness.

Set your alarm for fifteen minutes. Sit or kneel comfortably on a cushion or pillow. If it's more comfortable for your particular body, you can also do this meditation sitting in a chair with both feel flat on the floor. Stack your hands in your lap palms up. Sit up straight. Lengthen your spine. Slide your shoulder blades down your back so that your shoulders drop and your chest opens slightly. Close your mouth and place your tongue gently on the roof of your mouth behind your front teeth. (If your nose is congested, you can breathe through your mouth.) Close your eyes and bring your awareness to the physical sensation of the breath. Slow the cadence of your breath, lengthening the inhalation and the exhalation and adding a brief pause at the moment your lungs are full before you exhale and again when they are empty before you inhale. Begin to count your breaths. When you reach ten, begin again at one. Repeat this sequence of one to ten over and over.

Notice when you suddenly become aware that you are on eleven, twelve, or even thirty without having returned to one. This is an indication that your mind is wandering, and your presence has drifted along with it. That's okay; you haven't failed. It's all part of the training. Simply notice and begin again. And again. And again. One to ten.

Self-Pleasure with No Orgasm (Edging)

This exercise takes place daily over the course of one week. It's one of the most powerful gifts you will ever give yourself. By progressively increasing the breadth and depth of pleasurable sensation, you are increasing your body's capacity to hold sexual, or life-force, energy. Plan in advance. Block off your calendar. Consider it a retreat. Build a beautiful container—light candles, burn incense or diffuse essential oils, put on a sexy or ambient playlist, put devices away, and turn off notifications. Keep a journal with daily reflections of your experience.

Day One: Massage your feet for a full twenty minutes with coconut oil. Go slow. Take your time. Feel every square millimeter of your feet . . . the ball of your foot, the arch of your foot, the skin around each toenail, between each toe, around the ankle bones . . . Bring your awareness to the physical sensation of being touched. Honor your feet as your point of connection with the earth. Celebrate them with gratitude for the way they have carried and mobilized you all these years. Describe how it feels physically and emotionally.

Day Two: Massage your arms and legs for a full twenty minutes with coconut oil. Again . . . go slow. Take your time. Bring your awareness to the physical sensation of being touched. What is the sensation on your fingertips, the palm of your hand? What does the skin on your arms and legs feel like? Notice how it feels physically and emotionally.

Day Three: Extend your massage to your torso. Massage your belly, chest, breasts, nipples. This is a tender area. Slow it waaaayyyy down. Notice all the sensations under your fingers and hands. Also notice where else in your body you feel sensation that you aren't touching directly.

Day Four: Extend your touch to your whole body. Nothing is off-limits except your clitoris or frenulum. Imagine that you are touching your body for the first time—as if you are discovering new land, a paradise. Get curious. Imagine that in your exploration of this new land, you have happened upon a sacred temple—your genitals. This is where the universe lives in you. Embrace this perspective as you honor your body.

Day Five: Repeat Day Four.

Day Six: Today, explore your body entirely, *including your genitals*. This is where it gets tricky. The idea is that you are cultivating your body's capacity to hold energy. In order to do that, you cannot discharge the energy through orgasm. Go slow, draw out the arousal, and as you get closer to orgasm, back off, then build it back again. Play with the energy; it will feel spongy as it expands and contracts. See how long you can keep it going. Observe how your body feels as you ride the edge of orgasm without giving in. There's nowhere to go. You are just here in a heightened state of arousal. How much can you feel? How present can you be? What is your state of consciousness as you hold this energy? It can be hard to know when to stop. Plan to spend forty-five to sixty minutes. When it's time to complete the exercise, simply place one hand flat on your heart and the other on your genitals and apply gentle pressure. This should feel grounding and calming. If it's creating more arousal, move your hand from your genitals to your lower abdomen. Breathe slowly and deeply. Imagine the breath distributing life-force energy throughout your entire body from the top of your head to the tips of your toes. Visualize every cell in your body bathed in vibrancy, infused with life.

Day Seven: Repeat Day Six, but this time at the end of your session, you may choose to have an orgasm. If you do, feel the surrender to the full experience of sensation throughout your entire body. Imagine that the universe is making love to itself through you.

WITH OTHERS
Eye Gazing/Matching Breath

Set an alarm for twenty minutes. Both partners sit cross-legged on the floor, facing each other, with knees gently touching. If this is a difficult position for you to sit in, use pillows and blankets to provide support where needed. Alternatively, you can sit in two chairs or even lie down on your sides facing each other. Place your hands on each other's knees or forearms. Or simply allow your knees to be the only point of contact.

Gaze into each other's eyes without looking away.

You might feel awkward at first. That's okay. Let the discomfort express itself in whatever way it arises—laughter, fidgeting, diverting your gaze. Just let it out until you can finally relax. It can be difficult to figure out where to fix your gaze. Start by focusing on the space between your partner's eyes. As you relax into the practice, transfer your gaze to just one of their eyes. Every so often switch to their other eye and relax into a rhythm that feels comfortable. As soon as you notice you've lost eye contact, find your partner's gaze once again. Spend a few minutes slowing and synchronizing your breath. Silently negotiate a rhythm that is comfortable for both of you. Pause at the top of each inhalation and again at the bottom of each exhalation, creating moments of mutual stillness. Notice what happens as you become more and more present to each other and to yourselves.

Now look at the person in front of you as if you are looking at them for the first time. See them with fresh eyes. Imagine the day they were born, the moment they sprang from their mother's womb. Imagine their first breath, their first cry. Think about when they first learned to sit . . . and crawl . . . then walk . . . and run. Imagine them learning to navigate the world in their body, how to use their hands and feet. Imagine their first day of school, their favorite teacher, getting a good grade on a test, their happiest days, their biggest challenges. Think about their first experience of puberty—growing breasts, a first period, or a first wet dream. Imagine their experience of their own changing body. Perhaps they were excited, confused, embarrassed, scared. Think about all the places your partner has been that has led them to this moment, sitting here before you. Joy, discovery, risk, disappointment, heartache, self-esteem, shame. The highest highs and the lowest lows. As you look at your partner here in this moment, find appreciation for them on their journey. Look into their eyes and see the whole person.

Notice how it feels to see them fully . . . not just the parts you see as they relate to you, but the totality of their existence. And now notice how it feels to be fully seen by them.

Stay here for a few minutes in this moment of connection and appreciation. Bring your awareness alternately from fully seeing your partner and the experience of being fully seen. And finally, acknowledge your partner by placing a hand on your heart and bowing your head slightly, or, if it feels right, give each other a mutual hug.

Spend a Day Together in Silence

There is no better way to feel into the energy of a relationship than by spending a day together communicating without words. See what opportunities arise to notice the way your partner inhabits the space and communicates their thoughts and desires. If an entire day feels overwhelming, try five hours—or even three.

WITH THE WORLD

Eating a Meal Mindfully

Prepare and eat an entire meal with mindful awareness of each ingredient and the path it took to arrive on your plate and into your body. Seed to plant to flower to fruit to harvest to farmer to grocer to your kitchen. Experience the fullness of physical sensation of every morsel from chopping board to stove to plate to fork to mouth to belly. Bring your awareness to all five of your senses: How does your food look, feel, smell, sound, and taste? Find appreciation for the entirety of the world's participation in your meal.

Breathe in Life

Set a timer for fifteen minutes. Sit in a comfortable chair or on the floor. Simply bring your awareness to the physical sensation of your breath. When you find that your attention has drifted to your thoughts, simply notice and bring your awareness back to the physical sensation of your breath.

When you feel somewhat settled, begin to repeat these words on each inhalation:

I receive life as it comes to me.

And on each exhalation:

I let go.

Repeat this mantra over and over as you breathe mindfully. Notice the effect of these words on your physical body. What is the physical sensation of *receiving*? What is the physical sensation of *letting go*?

Continuing the repetition of the mantra in tandem with your breath, notice the energy in your body. What is the quality of the energy you feel when you *receive life as it comes to you*? What is the quality of the energy when you *let go*?

As you continue to breathe the mantra, notice the emotions of allowing life to flow through you. How does it feel to surrender?

When the timer sounds, stay in the experience for a few moments. Notice an openness, a trusting, a knowing, a sense of safety. Perhaps you can bring this feeling-sense with you to bed.

PART FIVE

CREATING SYNERGY

CHAPTER 13

THE WEAVING OF ALL PARTS

BY NOW, YOU'VE LIKELY HAD A COLLECTION OF POWERFUL EXPERI-ence and aha moments. Perhaps you are feeling open and excited or like something has clicked into place in a way that feels familiar and authentic. On the other hand, you might be feeling raw, vulnerable, conflicted, agitated, or a million other things. Whatever you are experiencing is normal and expected when you begin to look at yourself and your life a little differently. Dismantling belief systems and thought patterns can be disorienting. When one piece is dislodged, another goes with it, and before you know it, you and your surroundings are suddenly unrecognizable. It can feel like a cascade of breakdowns—like one of those intricate displays of sequentially tumbling dominoes—breathtaking and unstoppable.

Whether it feels pleasant or painful, empowering or uncomfortable, whether you call it positive or negative, whatever is coming up for you is okay—*you're* okay. The upheaval you feel results from the recognition of all the ways in which you have been out of integrity with yourself—the sudden awareness of the things you've pretended not to see and the realization that who you thought you were was simply someone else's idea that you internalized as your own adopted identity. This kind of shift in perception can be earth shattering in the way tectonic plates shift in an earthquake. Seemingly solid ground moves deep below the surface, often imperceptibly. Then suddenly and irreversibly, it alters the terrain on the surface. Now a chasm exists in what used to be a seamless expanse.

If this isn't disorienting enough, when your internal geography morphs, your relational landscape follows. It's not surprising that the people around you may resist your growth and transformation. It may not even be conscious. They simply may not be ready to face their own version of radical intimacy. You may very well need to evaluate your relationships and adjust your expectations and requirements. It might mean that some of your relationships will either evolve or maybe even be completed. Remember to take responsibility for the impact of your own growth and evolution on the people around you. If this sounds dramatic, it needn't be. What's the meme? People come into our lives for a reason, a season, or a lifetime. A substantial part of living a radically intimate life is noticing, discerning, and accepting the true nature of what is right in front of you and acting accordingly. As your support system shifts, you will need to rely even more heavily on your own internal resources to cultivate a radically intimate life.

There are a couple of concepts to consider that will support you in weaving all the parts of the Radical Intimacy Matrix. We talked about witness consciousness in Chapter 6 as part of emotional independence, but it's worth bringing up again in this context as it's a fundamental skill set for navigating radical intimacy. Witness consciousness is the awareness of your own thoughts, feelings, and emotions without judgment. In other words, it's the ability to simultaneously have the experience and observe yourself having the experience. As human beings we have a perpetual penchant for ascribing meaning to our experiences and the feelings that follow. The rose- or mud-colored glasses of subjective interpretation are blurred and refracted. Intrinsic in observing ourselves is the admission of a larger context, a possibility that what we perceive isn't necessarily a universal truth, that there are many lenses through which to see and interpret our world. Like the bumper sticker says: *Don't believe everything you think.*

Specifically in weaving all the parts together, invoking witness consciousness affords you the benefits of a meta-view, or bird's-eye view, of
where you are in the matrix. As you sit with the moral outrage of social
injustice, you might find perspective in *physical intimacy with yourself* on
your surfboard or yoga mat. When you are offended by the comments
of a family member, you might seek refuge in *energetic intimacy with
the world* under the stars and the remembrance of the vastness of the
universe. If you've suffered a conflict at work and you're particularly
anxious, you might skillfully soothe your nervous system by *physical
intimacy with another* by having a yummy night of sex. Witness consciousness is a powerful tool for providing the perspective, clarity,
agency, and choice in the way we observe, experience, and navigate all
the areas of our lives and work all nine areas of the matrix sequentially
and simultaneously.

Freedom and connection are also powerful concepts to explore in the
context of radical intimacy. I can't say enough about the importance of
infusing our relationships with personal space. The misunderstanding of
intimacy as an all-encompassing merging or enmeshment obliterates the
identity and self-awareness of the individuals. A well-defined sense of
self is essential to our *self-esteem* (what we think, feel, and believe about
ourselves), *self-worth* (the recognition that we are valuable human beings
deserving of love and belonging), and *self-confidence* (trust in our abilities,
qualities, and judgment). These are the very qualities that make it possible
to establish and maintain boundaries. If you think about it, two things
cannot come together unless they are actually two things. If they melt
into one entity, there is actually no longer a connection. Intimacy exists at
the interface or tessellation of two separate entities.

Another way to think about it is the way a tapestry is woven from individual threads. While the tapestry takes on the characteristics of one
seamless object, the individual threads that make it up maintain their
distinct existence. Unlike the ingredients of a cake, which dissolve into
each other in the synthesis of a new form, the woven threads of a tapestry
remain identifiable by color, texture, heft, and flexibility. Try to identify

the egg in a slice of sponge cake and you can't say the same thing. In your relationships, don't be the egg.

It's easy in the pursuit of intimacy to focus on the connection with another. There's nothing wrong with that. It's totally understandable. At its best, connection with another human being—physically, emotionally, and energetically—is healthy and life affirming and feels so damn good. And at the end of the day, so to speak, you must be willing to return to yourself. Skillful solitude is both a gift and an investment in yourself. Aloneness doesn't mean loneliness. If you cannot be with yourself, you will never be sure if you choose to connect out of desire or cling to a relationship out of desperation to be loved in a way you don't love yourself. Seek connection, yes; honor the freedom on which it is built.

The Radical Intimacy Matrix is a blueprint, a schematic for *Your-Name-Here 2.0*. Use it as a reference point for your experience, internal and external. The exercises in this book are a great way to intentionally navigate the nine areas of intimacy in the matrix. But really, at any given moment, no matter where you are or with whom, you may stop and reflect on where intimacy is alive. Some moments will live in more than one area at a time. For instance, imagine taking a first sip of coffee (or your preferred beverage). How many times have you poured yourself a cup and, before you knew it, your cup was empty, its former contents in your belly? Instead, what if you pause to inhale the aroma of freshly brewed coffee and notice the way the coffee swirls in the cup as you prepare it to your liking? Imagine becoming present to the sound of your mouth slurping to cool the hot liquid as it passes from the hard ceramic edge of the cup over your lips, filling your mouth. Finally, savor the taste of the coffee as it washes over your throat on its way to warm your belly. And now imagine the soil in which the coffee plant grew, the beans that ripened, the farmer who picked them, the person who operated the machines that roasted and packaged the beans. You have a moment of *physical intimacy with self* as your body responds to the stimulation of the coffee through the vehicle of your five senses. Also alive is a kind of *energetic intimacy with the world* in that you become aware of the people and the earth, sun, and rain that grew the plant that produced your beverage. Gratitude for what made it possible for you to have the privilege of this experience is an energy. And finally, if you are like me, perhaps you have a moment of *emotional intimacy with other* in that coffee is a passion I shared with my father. In fact, the five weeks he spent in hospice, laboring toward death, I made him several cups a day. As he grew weaker, he sipped it through a straw as I held it up to his mouth. In the last few days, when he was too weak to draw the coffee all the way up the straw, I held my finger over one end of the straw and dribbled it into his mouth like a hen feeding her hatchling. I don't think I am able to consume a single cup of coffee without the sweetness of love for my father and deep appreciation for the privilege of helping him prepare to shuffle off this mortal coil.

Transformation is rarely a straight trajectory. Evolution is iterative, and as we peel back one layer at a time to reveal more and more of our essential nature, our undeniable truth, it can be tricky to recognize obstacles and challenges for what they are. Each of us travels with a unique rucksack of history and conditions that affect the experience of our journey, through both nature and nurture. Common roadblocks to radical intimacy have been addressed along the way throughout the book so far, but here are ways in which they tend to show up in real life, along with ways to work with these challenges as they arise.

FEAR OF UNCERTAINTY

It's easy to recognize fear of uncertainty when it pertains to certain definable events. For instance, think about the anxiety we feel when a loved one is having a health crisis and we are waiting for the results of an emergency procedure. Another clearly recognizable way the fear of uncertainty manifests is when we apply for employment or admittance to a school or educational program and then wait to find out if we are "accepted" or "rejected." In all these cases, there exists a well-defined result we are hoping for. We approach these kinds of situations preloaded with a very good idea of what's at risk and what our desired outcome is. We can also point to fear of uncertainty in circumstances that affect our survival. Uncertainty of having your basic needs met—water, food, shelter, safety, justice—is intolerable and, of course, not an opportunity for self-development. However, many of us have a disdain for the kind of uncertainty that is normal and typical in the course of an otherwise stable life. You don't have to be a full-on control freak to worry about whether our date will go well, if we will be able to meet the challenges of our new position at work, or if our child's team will win their soccer match and if we will be able to comfort them skillfully if they don't. Our world is often ambiguous and unpredictable. Often, we focus on the thing we want at the exclusion of the possibility of that which we can't know.

When my first husband, Vic, and I were moving in together for the first time, we found a house to rent that we fell in love with. It was perfect for us—in fact, beyond our expectations given the limited budget of our twenty-five-year-old selves. We filled out an application and were thrilled to hear from the real-estate agent representing the owner that we had been approved. We were to meet him at the property the following day to put down our deposit and sign the lease. We talked all night about how to arrange the furniture, and the next day as we were heading out the door, we got a call. The owner changed his mind and decided to rent the house to someone else. We were devastated. Feeling sorry for us, the agent helped us find an apartment in the same area. It was charming and adequate, but we remained somewhat heartbroken. Exactly one month later, the house we lost burned to the ground. The tenants who had moved in survived but lost all their possessions. Because we rented in the same neighborhood and drove past our would-be house every day, we were able to see that by losing what we thought we wanted, we had been spared a loss much more profound. I carry this experience with me to this day as an example of surrendering gracefully to the not-knowing.

Think for a moment about the state of not-knowing. Buddhists call this *shoshin*, or "beginner's mind." When we approach any situation without preconceived notions, we are curious, open, and eager to learn something new. As notable Zen teacher Suzuki Roshi says, "In the beginner's mind there are many possibilities, in the expert's there are few." But we are not all Zen practitioners sitting on a cushion pondering our existence. Immersed in our busy lives, knowledge and expertise are reliable sources of our success. The challenge lies in developing the ability not only to tolerate a certain degree of ongoing uncertainty, but to embrace it as a gift of expansion and evolution. It's not that we shouldn't know *anything*, but that we can't know *everything*.

When you encounter anxiety of any sort, at the very moment you recognize that's what you're feeling, stop and retreat to a place to converse with yourself. Reflect on how you have shown up to relationships recently. Are you angry, critical, controlling, impatient? Are you withdrawn, uncommunicative, submissive, depressed? Think about the level of uncertainty in your life right now. Is it rooted in big issues like systemic racism, pandemics, global warming? Are you worried about your own well-being or that of your loved ones? Do you have concerns about where you will be five or ten years from now and what life will look like? Recognizing and naming your fear of uncertainty can give it context and support you in managing it skillfully so it doesn't come out sideways as you navigate your relationships. Once you acknowledge the uncertainty in your life and the ways in which it makes you feel vulnerable, you can simultaneously recognize and name what you do know, and can control, so you can set structures and containers for both.

FEAR OF THE TRUTH

The reason most of us tolerate situations that feel intolerable is because we are afraid of the truth. More accurately, we are afraid of what the truth means. If you've gotten this far in the book, you recognize that the way you thought, felt, believed about the world and your place in it has been shaped by the programming you received from your family, society, religion, advertising, entertainment, pornography, and other influences. In a practical sense, the process of becoming a person capable of radical intimacy is focused largely on unraveling the results of these influences and getting to the truth of who you really are underneath all the filters of conditioning. In doing so, fear of the truth is understandably a persistent source of anxiety along the way. You're dismantling what you thought was true and searching for what is actually true. The truth of who you are, how you feel, and what you think lives at the core of your being. If you've been living in accordance with the truth of your influencers, it is likely to feel you've been living a lie. Either in some small way or on some large scale, you've built a life that's misaligned with who you are. Understandably, seeing, saying, and stepping into the truth can be terrifying. What it means is that you will have to have some very hard conversations. Along with dismantling your own thought systems, you might need to dismantle the relationships that exist as a result, not to mention career, location, and other structures you based on beliefs that weren't yours. Here's the thing . . . it's more painful to continue to live a lie. You've embarked on this journey because you have been suffering in some kind of way in your current paradigm. The very root of that suffering is likely to be that you've been alienated from your truth. And the truth of seeing the truth is that once you recognize it, you can't unsee it.

So, what's one to do when gripped by fear of the truth? The answer is simple. Do nothing. On the path of transformation, when you touch the marrow of your own existence, it is imperative that you focus on *being* with your new awareness rather than *doing* something about it. Eventually, you will need to make some changes, but there are a million ways in which that might play out. My mantra for times like this is *No sudden moves.* It may mean sitting in the discomfort for a while to sort through all the possibilities for rebuilding your life in accordance with your truth, but as author and podcaster Glennon Doyle says, "We can do hard things." Take the time you need to meet your new reality internally before you jump to fixing your external reality to match.

INTOLERANCE FOR DISCOMFORT

When French Cuban American writer and eroticist Anaïs Nin wrote, "And the day came when the risk to remain in a tight bud was more painful than the risk it took to blossom," she was talking about the benefits of tolerating discomfort. Growth is uncomfortable. Magic happens outside your comfort zone. There are a million ways to say it. You can stay the same, or you can transform yourself and your life. Cultivating the deeply connected relationships you desire—with yourself, others, and the world—requires all kinds of discomfort. It's as simple as that. It's not that feeling less than comfortable is the goal, but with growth as the goal, it's a necessary part of the process. And it's easy to fall into the resistance of feeling less than comfortable, especially in the techno-industrial era, when there are a myriad of ways to distract ourselves.

LACK OF NOVELTY

One of the most common complaints I hear from partners in a long-term monogamous relationship is that they are bored. This shows up primarily in the realm of physical intimacy, but emotional intimacy can also feel stale over time. Often, when I dig deeper, I find that there is little in the way of imagination and experimentation being employed to create new and novel experiences.

Author Saul Bellow says in *The Adventures of Augie March*, "Boredom is the conviction that you can't change . . . the shriek of unused capacities."

There are infinite ways and places in which to have sex, and there are a myriad of sources for inspiration in finding creative ways to infuse new experiences into a relational dynamic—from erotica to toys to kink to role play. Boredom is a choice.

LACK OF MYSTERY

When we have spent a long time with a partner, it's easy to think we know everything about them. First of all, with an attitude of curiosity, there's always something new to learn about someone else—and ourselves, for that matter. Additionally, most of what we think we know is rooted in assumptions predicated on history. There's a funny trick that I often assign couples dealing with too much time together (hello pandemic). Go on a first date. Forget you know each other at all and plan an evening together in which you pretend you are meeting for the first time. Try seeing your partner with fresh eyes. Ask all about them and pay attention to their answers. Notice the energy between you. Observe both your partner and yourself as you open the doorway of discovery.

Another way to cultivate mystery in your relational dynamic is role play. Each of you creates a new persona, then you meet in public or in the bedroom and see what happens.

TOO BUSY/TIRED/STRESSED

Modern life can be exhausting. Combined with our busy, hyperstimulating, multitasking lifestyle, this makes many of us both physically and mentally exhausted. At the end of the day, in the argument for sleep or sex, sleep often wins. Making time for soul-nourishing intimacy is important to the health of a relationship, as well as each individual partner. Sometimes it's just hard to get started on something, but once we do, we are swept away by how easy it is. Sex can be that way. Make a request of your partner to kiss or touch a specific area of your body that you know to be an erogenous zone. Push past resistance you might feel and bring your awareness to the physical sensation of what you are experiencing. Imagine that one small area of pleasure growing. Visualize it as honey or melted chocolate flowing and swirling through your entire body, bringing warm, delicious pleasure as it wakes you up to the possibility of soul-nourishing sex.

You also might try shifting your story about sex. We often forget that sex is something we do for ourselves, seeing it as something we do for our partner. We also tend to think of sex as draining, when in fact the hormones and neurotransmitters secreted during sex are actually energizing and nourishing to our bodies and brains. In addition, our pelvic muscles and genital tissues benefit greatly from the additional blood flow that occurs during sex. When we shift our story of sex from something that is an obligation that depletes us to something that is an essential form of nourishment, we are more inspired to find energy for it.

MORAL OUTRAGE

Moral outrage is a felt sense of anger and disgust in response to a perceived moral violation. When skillfully managed and regulated, it can be a useful and productive perspective, energizing and motivating ethical activism. However, moral outrage has the capacity to be self-serving, divisive, and addictive. There is plenty to be outraged about when engaging with the world at large. A myriad of varied sociopolitical, climate, and humanitarian issues inspire fierce and polarized perspectives. To cultivate intimacy with the world, it's imperative that we employ emotional skill as well as presence, humility, and curiosity.

As my own teacher Roshi Joan Halifax says about moral outrage in her book *Standing at the Edge: Finding Freedom Where Fear and Courage Meet*, "Shaming, blaming, and self-righteousness put us in a superior power position, which can feel satisfying in the short term but isolates us from others in the long term." She goes on, "In the final analysis, I have learned that moral outrage can have beneficial or harmful consequences not only for ourselves but for our relationships and even our society. Our discernment, insight into our intentions, and our ability to regulate our emotions are what make the difference in whether moral outrage serves or not."

EXISTENTIAL EXHAUSTION

My most desperate moments of energetic decimation have brought me to this realization: there are two varieties of exhaustion. *Physical* exhaustion is the kind of fatigue that shows up when we haven't fed, watered, moved, or rested our bodies in the way that sustains our well-being. Typical symptoms are sleepiness, brain fog, headache, muscle weakness, short-term memory loss, and difficulty regulating mood. *Existential* exhaustion is what I call the syndrome that occurs at a certain point in the downward spiral of compounded physical exhaustion when there is no clear path out of the current paradigm. Common symptoms include feeling overwhelmed, depression, lack of motivation, loss of purpose, disorientation, and hopelessness. Times of severe depletion like this are ripe for calamity like accidents and illness. Often, it's the only thing that stops the action and imposes the space for rest. If this sounds familiar, the prevention or remedy can be to rebalance the matrix. Existential exhaustion happens when there is an overabundance of outward focus at the expense of intimacy with self. It's also indicative of too much doing and not enough being. No matter how hard it seems, carve out some time to slow down and breathe. Enlist the help of family and friends to support you in taking a few moments for yourself. Take a look at your commitments and be realistic about what is sustainable. Find time for moments of joy. Sometimes that means changing what you do, and sometimes it means changing the way you do it. No matter what your circumstances, your need for rest is real and required.

There are infinite possibilities for working the principles of radical intimacy in just as many combinations. Whether you focus on each of the nine individual areas or how a single experience can traverse several areas at once, it's bound to be a fruitful endeavor and one that connects you deeply to yourself while increasing your capacity for connection with others. Remember my experience of the symphony? Each of us is the conductor of our life—cuing the playful frolic of the woodwinds and the curious contemplation of the cellos, summoning the soulful sorrow of the violins, and egging on the escalating conviction of the timpani and the confrontational crash of cymbals. You may love the sound of a violin, but not so much a tuba, but the point is not to take only the parts you favor. The deep brass anchors the whole in a way that would cause imbalance were it missing. All the parts are valid and needed. Each plays an essential role. A symphony of flutes, piccolos, and oboes alone would lack the kind of depth provided only by a contrabass or a baritone saxophone. In the same way, our experience of physical intimacy with a lover is anchored by our emotional intimacy with ourselves. The excruciating pain of loss is tempered by the affection of a beloved pet or a good friend. And conversely, that sweetness is made more exquisite because we know the contrast of heartache. Just like the symphony, the whole becomes greater than the sum of its parts and takes on a life of its own as the unimaginable perfection of an intricately woven tapestry.

CHAPTER 14

SUSTAINING RADICAL INTIMACY

NTIMACY IS A PRACTICE. THERE IS A DIFFERENCE BETWEEN AN EXER-
cise and a practice. The exercises I've included thus far are intended to
facilitate powerful experiences in which you bring what you understand
cognitively to a felt sense of embodiment of those same concepts. Exercises are impactful; they are one-off or occasional activities that are
intended to inspire deep shifts in the way you see, feel, sense, and understand your reality. Not every exercise moves internal, relational, or
systemic mountains, but the essence of an exercise is an expedition into
the unknown with an attitude of curiosity and adventure.

You'll notice that in this chapter, I include practices rather than exercises. If the purpose of an exercise is awakening, a practice is intended to
further transformation and to sustain the shift. You might calendar one
specific time to do an exercise—like a penis massage or an evening spent
engaged with the Wheel of Emotion. A practice is designed to be incor-
porated into the fabric of your day that supports your new way of being.

For instance, brushing your teeth with your nondominant hand forces a kind of mindfulness not needed when you tackle a task by rote. One yoga class is an exercise; twice a week for a couple of months becomes a practice. You might have a mind-blowing experience in that one class that opens a new perspective of some kind. You might even describe that experience as life altering, but it's a practice that supports you in sustaining the new perspective and living your life from this new level of consciousness. If you wear glasses, think of a visit to the optometrist when they put that big machine up to your eyes and have you look at an eye chart through a series of combinations of lenses. You know, "A or B? A . . . or B?" That moment when all of a sudden, the smudge in the bottom line takes the shape of a Z. "OMG, I can see!" you exclaim. The experience of seeing something you couldn't previously see is an aha moment of awakening. But you don't carry around your eye doc and their equipment as you navigate your life. You employ a pair of glasses to support you in seeing the Z in the smudge on an ongoing basis. The annual visit to the doctor is the exercise. The glasses are the practice.

A cognitive or embodied epiphany is exciting and compelling. The impact is often memorable and profound when a new way of being reveals itself in the moment. A vision of a new way needs time and care to develop and grow. A new way of *being* requires new ways of *doing*. It's through careful and sustained nurturance that radical intimacy takes shape over time. Stay the course.

STILLNESS

The best thing you can do to cultivate intimacy in your life is to start with yourself. On a daily basis, sit down, shut up, and listen. Whether it's Zazen-style or any other kind of meditative tradition, a dedicated stillness practice is the most courageous and powerful thing you can do not only for your own well-being, but also for the well-being of your relationships. Commit to this every single day. The amount of time you sit is not as important as the consistency with which you do it. I recommend a minimum of twenty minutes per day. If you are not a seasoned meditator, you can work up to that by starting with one minute and gradually increasing it over time. There's an old Zen saying, "You should sit in meditation for twenty minutes every day, unless you are too busy. In that case, you should sit for an hour."

REGULAR ACTS OF RANDOMNESS

Doing these simple things on a semiregular basis—say, once every week or two—is a powerful way to build presence and curiosity. When we do things by rote, our mind is elsewhere while we go through the motions. Approaching regular tasks differently forces us to pay attention to what we are doing in a way not normally required. Drive a different route home. Sleep with your head at the foot of the bed. Like that episode of *Seinfeld* where George turns his life around by doing the opposite of what his intuition tells him, have yourself an Opposite Day in which you make small choices throughout the day that are the opposite of what you would usually choose.

RANDOM ACTS OF INTIMACY

Seek opportunities to ask the people who you encounter throughout your day how they are doing, make an observation, or offer them a compliment. Your neighbor, mail carrier, barista . . . We tend to think of intimacy as deep, vast, and profound. Sometimes we need a big meal, and sometimes a snack is the perfect amount of nourishment. Regular bite-size moments of intimacy strung together over a long period of time deepen our overall experience of life by providing reference points of vulnerability and connection.

TOUCH YOUR GENITALS EVERY DAY

Touch your genitals every single day—not for pleasure, but for power. Culturally, there is so much shame and taboo around this part of our bodies that with the exception of showering and urinating, we can go weeks without acknowledging their presence. Simply place your hand on your genitals and take a few breaths. Honor and celebrate the role they play in your overall wellness. **Note:** If you are someone for whom it is not empowering to touch your genitals, it is okay to simply skip this exercise.

RETREAT DAYS

Schedule a quarterly retreat day in which you let people in your life know in advance that you will be unavailable and unresponsive to digital communication and otherwise. This might be impossible for you given your circumstance. If you cannot carve out an entire day, even an hour or two can be healing and restorative. Spend the time taking care of yourself in whatever ways are powerful for you. Perhaps it's a moment of rest, or even sleep. Maybe it's getting lost in a creative project or reading that book you haven't had time for. You might take a trip to a favorite spot in nature. Step away from devices, conversation, responsibilities, schedules, friends, and family. Unplug and disengage. Focus on being rather than doing. You might consider not speaking during your retreat as well. If so, carry around a pad and pen if you leave your home. If you are in a relationship, you might plan one partnered retreat for every two solo retreats you schedule.

WALK BAREFOOT

Kiss the earth with your feet at regular intervals as a practice. Follow the guidance in "Exercises for Cultivating Physical Intimacy with the World." **Note:** If it's not possible for you to stand or walk, you can achieve the same benefits by sitting or lying down directly on grass, sand, or on a blanket. If you cannot or do not want to make physical contact with the ground, simply being outdoors will suffice.

SELF-PLEASURE

One of the most powerful ways to get and stay deeply connected to yourself is to engage in self-pleasure on a regular basis—even if you are having partnered sex. Whatever the cadence (weekly, biweekly, monthly), follow the self-pleasure guidance in "Exercises for Cultivating Physical Intimacy with Self."

MINDFUL SHOWERING

Showering is a practice in and of itself. As an exercise in sensual awareness, you make it an opportunity to build intimacy with yourself and the environment of your bathroom. Bringing your full attention to all the sensations of your body while you shower strengthens your ability to be present in other areas of your life. Showering is one example of taking advantage of something to do on a regular basis and turning it into a mindfulness practice. Other ideas are getting dressed, brushing your teeth, cooking dinner, washing dishes, or going for an evening walk. Pick one and make it a regular mindfulness practice.

MORNING WAKING RITUAL

You know the precious morning moments when we first open our eyes, our minds clear, and our perspective is fresh? Well, 23 percent of us grab our phones within sixty seconds of waking, with another 34 percent waiting five to ten minutes. If this sounds like you, consider adopting a morning waking ritual that incorporates presenting yourself to your environment one sense at a time. Begin by coming to consciousness, either organically or by alarm, and positioning yourself comfortably on your back. Gently lengthen you spine and limbs, taking long, slow, deep breaths. Imagine you are breathing in life-force energy and exhaling slumber. Spend one full minute focusing on each sense one at a time. What is the quality of light in the room? What is the temperature of the room, and how do the sheets feel on your skin? What do you hear, taste, and smell? Consider extending this mindfulness throughout your morning before you pick up your devices.

HUGGING PRACTICE

Hugging for partners is a simple and powerful way to connect. I haven't met a single couple who wouldn't benefit from a hugging practice. It's easy to do and requires very little time or effort. Once a day, stop what you are doing and make thirty seconds of uninterrupted eye contact followed by a one-minute hug. Breathe together slowly and deeply, matching the cadence of inhalations and exhalations. That's it. Easy-peasy lemon squeezy. For bonus points: do this twice a day, morning and evening.

RELATIONSHIP CHECK-INS

Set a time, once a week, to come together and talk about your relationship. It doesn't have to be big and heavy. This kind of maintenance decreases the chances that it will get big and heavy, like an elephant in the room. Set a regular day and time to sit down together. Ask each other and yourself three questions: What is working well in our relationship? What could we be doing better? What is one theme we can focus on this week? Examples: Joy, Connection, Empathy, Support, Adventure, Humor.

LOVE NOTES

Keep a supply of Post-its® on hand to write each other, or yourself, weekly love notes. If you're having trouble thinking of what to write, simply name one thing you witness that week that you admire about your partner. If you are flying solo, write one thing you admire about yourself. Really!

EYE GAZE

Chances are you don't make very much sustained eye contact with your partner. Meeting each other in this way primarily cultivates energetic intimacy, but emotional and physical intimacy often follows. I recommend weekly sessions as a practice. Follow the guidance in "Exercises for Cultivating Energetic Intimacy with Others."

SKY GAZE

You don't have to be a meteorologist or an astronomer to enjoy gazing at the day or night sky. Spending twenty to forty minutes once a week communing with the clouds or the stars is a powerful practice that will give you context for your small part in a much greater story.

KNOW YOUR CITY

Get intimate with the city in which you reside. Explore places you haven't yet visited. Read about various communities and the ways in which they are challenged and thriving. Patronize local stores and restaurants in appreciation of the efforts of your neighbors. Technology makes the global community smaller, but there are power and comfort in staying connected to the people close at hand. Set a time once a month to explore a different part of your physical surroundings. For instance, declare the first Sunday of each month "City Sunday" and make it a practice.

SERVE YOUR COMMUNITY

Adopt one way to serve your community. It doesn't always take a lot of time or money to have a big impact. Volunteer in some way that improves the lives of the people or animals that coexist with you. You might work through the structure of an existing organization or contribute to projects with which you are aligned. Allocating your resources for the benefit of others in need brings a profound sense of satisfaction and purpose through the acknowledgment that we are all deeply connected on some level. None of us is free until all of us are free.

POP YOUR BUBBLE

Learn about the lived experience of people outside your specific demographic. There are tons of books available and infinite resources online that detail what it's like to live in a body or circumstances different from your own. Understanding what other people are dealing with broadens our perspective of how to care for each other and begins to dismantle systems that oppress or victimize members of our human family.

TAKE UP A CAUSE

Antiracism, climate change, human rights, save-the-manatee, world hunger, reproductive rights, human trafficking . . . the list goes on and on. Find one thing you are passionate about and become an expert. Take a stand; speak up for the kind of justice you want to see in the world. Inspire, impress, and influence. Contribute to the conversation.

TRAUMA-RESPONSE TOOL KIT FOR CALMING AND SELF-REGULATION

The following exercises are often used to calm an activated nervous system and mitigate a trauma response. I encourage you to seek the support of a trauma-informed therapist or a practitioner specializing in somatic experiencing as needed.

THREE-PART BREATH

Sit comfortably on the floor or in a chair with your feet on the floor. Straighten your spine and relax your shoulders. This exercise can also be done lying down or in whatever position is comfortable for your body, as needed.

1. Inhale through your nose, allowing your belly to gently expand as the breath moves into your lungs. Then exhale slowly through your nose or through pursed lips, tightening your abdominal muscles and drawing your navel to your spine. Empty your lungs as much as possible.
2. Repeat with an additional step. Inhale through the nose, allowing your belly to expand, and then allow the breath to expand your rib cage as well. Exhale slowly through your nose or pursed lips. Squeeze the air out of your rib cage and belly completely.
3. Take it one step further. Inhale through your nose, once again, allowing your belly and rib cage to expand. Then invite the breath into your upper chest, stretching your pectoral muscles all the way

up to your clavicle. Then slowly exhale fully through your nose or pursed lips.

BOX BREATHING

This can be done anytime, anywhere. Inhale to the count of four. Hold to the count of four. Exhale to the count of four. Hold to the count of four. Repeat.

ORIENTING

Take a moment and bring attention to your *physical* comfort in this Somatic Experiencing® technique. Sit comfortably on the floor or in a chair with your feet on the floor. Straighten your spine and relax your shoulders. This exercise can also be done lying down if needed.

1. Take a moment and notice your overall experience.
2. Move your feet, shifting them around until you feel a strong connection to the floor.
3. Notice the way your back and thighs feel on the chair. Feel how the chair supports you.
4. Adjust your body so that you feel comfortable. Take a few moments to be with the feeling of being supported by the chair and stabilized by the floor.
5. Now, look around your surroundings and notice something that feels resourceful—for example, a tree outside the window, the art on the wall, a calming color, the clock on the desk, etc. Spend a few moments observing the resource. Notice how it feels to feel connected to this resource.
6. What do you notice *now* about your overall comfort—physically and emotionally?

5-4-3-2-1 SENSES TECHNIQUE

Bring your awareness to your breath. Do your best to lengthen and deepen your breathing. When you find your breath, begin these five steps:

1. Acknowledge five things you can see (floor, book, spot on the wall, etc.).
2. Acknowledge four things you can touch (pillow, your hair, a friend's hand, etc.).
3. Acknowledge three things you can hear (air-conditioning fan, car driving by, clock ticking, etc.).
4. Acknowledge two things you can smell (soap, flowers, candle, etc.)
5. Acknowledge one thing you can taste (the inside of your mouth, a piece of candy, a sip of a beverage, etc.).

Note: If you are someone with a disability that prevents you from engaging one or more of your five senses, simply skip that step.

ACKNOWLEDGMENTS

It's been my lifelong dream to write and publish a book. In fact, my mother has in her possession several early attempts from my childhood, including a narrative nonfiction work on Hemingway and another one on hemorrhoids—both complete with my own illustrations. I come from a long line of book people, and it is with gratitude and humility that I contribute this title to the literary space. Everywhere I've ever been has led me to where I am today, and I could legitimately thank everyone I've ever met. There are, however, a group of individuals who have directly supported the birth of this book or helped shape the version of me who finally sat down and wrote about intimacy. It's with profound appreciation that I thank the following people.

To my clients, for trusting me with the most tender and vulnerable parts of themselves. It's an honor to support you on your journey. I see you. I got you. I love you.

To my brilliant editor, Renée Sedliar, for embracing my voice and my work wholeheartedly while asking all the right questions. This book exists as it does because of your collaboration.

To my dear agents, Jan Baumer and Steve Troha, thank you for seeing me, choosing me, loving me, and smacking me in the head when needed. I won the agent lottery. Twice.

To Alison Dalafave, Amanda Kain, Amber Morris, Annette Wenda, and the rest of the teams at Hachette Go and Folio Literary, gratitude abounds.

To Juliet Percival, whose beautiful artwork graces these pages. What a joyful experience to find you across the globe in the middle of a pandemic and collaborate so intimately. The love and care with which you created these images is palpable and appreciated.

To Azure Antoinette, your beautiful soul, brilliant mind, and brave heart inspire me every damn day. Thank you for letting me borrow your consciousness.

To Cassius Adair and Sylveon Consulting, for reading and reflecting back to me, with sensitivity and kindness, all the places I might have unintentionally caused harm.

To Kelly Notaras, Nirmala Nataraj, Annie Wylde, and the team at KN Literary Arts, I couldn't put a book out into the world without your hands on it. Thank you for your early and essential shepherding of my vision.

To my loving and devoted husband, Andrew—the Ben Wyatt to my Leslie Knope—you teach me every day what real partnership means. Thank you for loving me in such a way that I feel free, and for all you've done to support me through this endeavor. I love you, Plums.

To my son, Oliver, for being my own personal ultra, your love and encouragement are everything. Vamos Galaxy!

To my daughter, Rachel, for keeping me relevant and for continuing to let me be your mom even though more than half the time now it's *you* leading the way. To Chris Seddon for loving our girl and letting her love you back, you're the best son-in-law.

To my mom, Bobbie Korstvedt, for your impeccable proofreading, editorial feedback, and personal musings along the way. What a gift it is to share this process with you.

To Vic Hennegan, for the decades of navigating this life together in one form or another. This is surely not the first time, nor will it be the last.

To Isharna Walsh, for your leadership, partnership, and friendship. It's a joy to be a part of the Coral universe. I admire and adore you beyond measure. To Amy Marie Slocum and Agatha French, my content cocreators and fellow wordsmiths, Dude. To Amy Neumann, and the rest of the Coral team, for being a bunch of bighearted badasses.

To my beloved friend and colleague Marnie Breecker, for your trust, love, and respect. To the team at the Center for Relational Healing, Jaclyn Schwartz, Kim Gould, Lisa Palac, John McNamara, and Beth Tiras, thank you for accepting me as one of your own. It's a privilege to work with such a committed and heartful team of clinicians. To Helping Couples Heal and Duane Osterlind, for your patience and for lending me your left brain as needed.

To my colleagues Ian Kerner, Holly Richmond, Kristen Mark, Elaine and David Taylor-Klaus, Habeeb Akande, and Kate Anthony, for your professional prowess and personal loveliness.

To Sridhar Silberfein, for years of love, laughter, devotion, and other shenanigans.

To Amy V. Dewhurst, for your sustained enthusiasm for meeting me in the spaces between contexts with grit, grace, and ingenuity. Radhe, Radhe!

To Katie Brauer, for your endless love, wisdom, and hilarity. You are a legend in every sense of the word.

To my friend and angel Dale Rodrigues, for so generously supporting me, my family, and my work. I love the way you see me.

To Alex Soojung-Kim Pang, for being at the other end of my distraction device when I need you. That I can always count on you for solid, smart, and oft-hilariously delivered perspective keeps me tethered to what matters most. Your integrity and flexibility are not lost on me.

There are some spectacular women whose sisterhood nourishes my heart and soul and reminds me who I am. Jodi Goodman, Patricia Sullivan-Rothberg, Kayla Locklin, Catherine Just, Deborah Boelsen, Kasey Luber, Lily Dulan, Felicia Tomasko, Kim Bonheim, Jonalyn Morris Busam, Kathy Jonas, Staci Anderson, Laura Rexer, and Naomi Cooper Hochman, I love each of you truly, madly, deeply, to the moon and back.

To Brian Becker, Tom Freund, Neil Berg, Matt Hudson, and Ken Bloom, for your love, creativity, and sustained friendship.

To my friend and high school English teacher Ann Singer, your passion for literature and Tab® were contagious. Thank you for instilling in me an appreciation of Moby's Dick in spite of myself.

To Katherine Alcorn, devoted adviser of the Tappan Zee High School Women's Coalition, for your dedication to rooting a generation of young women in the history of the movement and for sharing your own brand of practical feminism so freely.

To the founder of Emerging Women, Chantal Pierrat, for curating a courageous community of changemakers. I'm ever so grateful for your ongoing support and nurturance.

To Ron Martino, Bethany Gillan, and the crew at Magical Threads Co. and Residence 11, for your generosity and commitment to the conversation.

To Ashley Diana and Alex King, for the infusion of energy, creativity, motivation, and love on a regular basis.

To my soul siblings Sarah and Steven Marshank, for always being a soft place to land. You inspire me in so many ways, and I love you with every cell in my body.

To my first love, Danny Kosarin, I'm thoroughly grateful for our friendship of a lifetime and the gift of Lauren and Kira.

To Psalm Isadora, for walking your dirty-ass bare feet straight into my life and changing everything. To Rachael Hensley, Miriam Elyse, Julianne Reynolds, Colin Earl, Katie Shaw, Lillian Love, Monique Caulfield, Esi Wildcat, Julian Picaza, Byron Bliss, Anka Malatynska, Corissa Bragg, and the rest of the Shakti Kula, you are my life force. Aim Hreem Shreem.

To Krishna Das, Shiva Baum, Narayan Zalben, Nina Rao, Mark and Mary Gorman, David Nichtern, Raghu Markus, Saraswati Markus, Bruce Margolin, Mohan Baum, Michael Brian Baker, Govind Das and Radha Rosen, Clay Campbell, Rhiannon Roze, Saul David Raye, Adam Bauer, Mirabai Starr, Mike Crall, Dassima Murphy, Gagan and Jyoti Levy, Maegen Andersen and John Phaneuf, Srutih Asher Colbert, Julie Devi Hale, Annapurna Alisa Sydell, Maureen Ananda, Mary Godschalk, and the entire NKB Satsang, the whole *mishpocha*, my life is richer for your generosity and loving awareness. Ram Ram.

Deep bow to my beloved teacher Roshi Joan Halifax and the Upaya Zen Center Sangha for the unfathomable work you do in the world to alleviate suffering. To Kozan Palevsky, Kigaku Rossetter, and Monshin Overley, for your loving guidance and friendship.

To the staff of Caring House, for allowing me the opportunity to contribute to the cultivation of a beautiful and dignified end-of-life experience. And to the residents, for allowing me the privilege of knowing you and caring for you in your most vulnerable moments.

To Deva Premal and Miten, for the sweetness of your love even at a distance and for being the abiding embodiment of mantra no matter what.

To Jade Luna, Jerome Braggs, Sir Rucifer, and Chani Nicholas, for introducing me to myself in ways that, left to my own devices, I may never have found.

To my gurus Alan Watts, Ram Dass, Maharaj-ji Neem Karoli Baba, Guruji Sri Amritananda Natha Saraswati, Aiya Chaitanyananda Natha Saraswati, and Amma Sri Mata Amritanandamayi Devi, pranams at your feet.

To my beloved Hudson River for providing an exquisite backdrop for the first twenty-five years of my life. I would not be who I am without your profound influence on how I see and feel the world and my place in it.

And finally, to all the lovers I've ever had, for joining me in my laboratory of intimacy. Thanks for playing along.

INDEX

Note: Page numbers in *italics* indicate illustrations.

Scan the QR code to access free audio clips provided by our partners at Coral. These audio exercises pair with the "Shift Your Self Pleasure" scripts that begin on page 136 of *Radical Intimacy*.

SCAN HERE OR VISIT THE LINK BELOW

hach.co/3tIydtr

Coral

Real people need help sustaining real intimacy. Join the hundreds of thousands of people using Coral to cultivate fun, healthy, and deeply connected relationships.

Find out more at getcoral.app